More Praise for

WHO'S AFRAID TO BE A MILLIONAIRE?

"*Who's Afraid to Be a Millionaire?* helps readers understand how to successfully play the great financial game of life. Mr. Boston makes the notion of wealth building practical and feasible for even the most economically challenged."

> —MARY JANE M. SEEBACH
> Managing Director Public Affairs
> Countrywide

"Kelvin Boston hits the nail on the head with his no-nonsense approach to financial empowerment. *Who's Afraid to Be a Millionaire?* offers sound and reasonable tips for anyone seeking to secure their financial future."

> —CHERYL McDONALD
> Vice President
> Diverse Growth Segments
> Wells Fargo

"Kelvin Boston's approach to wealth building is thoughtful, inspiring, and holistic. *Who's Afraid to Be a Millionaire?* will surely be a blessing to many."

> —GLINDA BRIDGFORTH
> Founder, Bridgforth Financial
> and co-author of *Girl, Make Your Money Grow!*

WHO'S AFRAID TO BE A MILLIONAIRE?

WHO'S AFRAID TO BE A MILLIONAIRE?

7-80

Mastering Financial and Emotional Success

KELVIN E. BOSTON

WILEY

John Wiley & Sons, Inc.

Published by John Wiley & Sons, Inc., Hoboken, New Jersey.
Published simultaneously in Canada.

For general information on our other products and services or for technical support, please contact our Customer Care Department within the United States at (800) 762-2974, outside the United States at (317) 572-3993 or fax (317) 572-4002.

Wiley also publishes its books in a variety of electronic formats. Some content that appears in print may not be available in electronic books. For more information about Wiley products, visit our web site at www.wiley.com.

Library of Congress Cataloging-in-Publication Data:

Boston, Kelvin E.
  Who's afraid to be a millionaire? : mastering financial and emotional success / Kelvin E. Boston.
     p. cm.
  "Published simultaneously in Canada."
  Includes index.
  ISBN-13: 978-0-470-06799-4 (cloth)
  ISBN-10: 0-470-06799-3 (cloth)
1. Finance, Personal—United States.   2. Investments—United States.   3. Success—Psychological aspects.   I. Title.
  HG179.B5848   2006
  332.024′01—dc22

                                                                          2006017993

Printed in the United States of America.

10 9 8 7 6 5 4 3 2 1

To my God; my mother, Astor Boston; my father, Arthur Money; my family members; my business associates; my coworkers; my friends. And to all who have inspired and encouraged me to complete this book.

Consult not your fears, but your hopes and your dreams.
Think not about your frustrations, but about your
unfulfilled potential; Concern yourself not with what you
tried and failed in, but with what is still possible for you to do.

—*Pope John XXIII*

CONTENTS

FOREWORD

Money is more than an economic necessity. It is one of the most powerful motivators of human behavior. It taps into the deepest layers of our personalities and sets off powerful emotional charges. Our attitudes about money influence our behavior, aspirations, and emotional reactions to ourselves, our families, and our friends. Still, as central as money is to our everyday lives, few Americans fully understand how our monetary attitudes shape our financial success.

When I began specializing in money psychology and money conflict resolution in my psychotherapy practice in 1983 in Washington, DC, almost nothing had been written about the subject. Over the years, countless investment guides have been written, but only a few have explored the relationship between emotional attitudes and financial success. This is why, as an author, money psychology writer, money coach, and therapist, I welcome Kelvin Boston's *Who's Afraid to Be a Millionaire?*

Is financial fear keeping you from financial success? This is the major question Kelvin Boston helps readers answer in *Who's Afraid to Be a Millionaire?* Financial fear and net worth generally go hand in hand. If you have a fear of achieving financial success, taking financial risks, or taking responsibility for your financial life, you're apt to have a low net worth. And if you do not have such fears or have overcome them, then you're apt to have a high net worth.

In *Who's Afraid to Be a Millionaire?* Kelvin shows readers how understanding their financial fears will help them increase their net worth. Based on his popular wealth-building seminars, writings, and experience as a financial journalist, this valuable resource guide helps readers understand the emotional and financial steps associated with personal economic success. You may wonder if Americans are really afraid of financial success. Are many of us afraid of taking financial risks or making financial decisions?

The answer is yes. I know because, in my work, I have helped countless individuals deal with these and other financial anxieties.

Some financial researchers believe that financial worries are a natural by-product of living in a capitalistic society. Today, however, Americans must face the economic realities of living in the twenty-first century. Many Americans have never had to cope with a post 9/11, terrorist-alerted society at home and a competitive global economy abroad. We have never been forced, as a nation, to take control of our future retirement needs nor been offered so many financial services to do so. Today, Americans must make major credit, housing, and investment decisions for their households while preparing to face the economic challenges associated with a national savings deficit, trade deficit, and income deficit. These factors suggest why Kelvin refers to this era as "an age of financial anxiety."

His *Who's Afraid to Be a Millionaire?* is a timely resource guide for individuals interested in securing financial success in this time of financial anxiety—not just because of the practical financial information it provides, but because it helps people understand the connection between their financial success and their financial fear.

When it comes to overcoming fears, knowledge is power. This is another reason Kelvin Boston's *Who's Afraid to Be a Millionaire?* is so valuable. This book can offer you the financial knowledge you need to overcome your financial fears. Today, many Americans need such power to have an honest discussion about how their financial fear is influencing their financial behavior and decision making. This book also provides useful information on credit management, financial planning, buying life insurance, home ownership, investing in mutual funds, retirement planning, and how to start a business. In an age of financial anxiety, this sound information is what many Americans need to move beyond their financial fears.

Accumulating a million-dollar net worth will not in itself make you feel financially successful. While the financial strategies in this book will help you build a seven-figure net worth, you should remember that Kelvin uses the word millionaire as a metaphor for financial success. Financial success, Kelvin explains is really about economic freedom and having the ability to make personal lifestyle choices. Many Americans need to see at least a million dollars in their net worth to feel financially successful, while others do not. Still, neither group will feel financially secure until they understand that they are the "masters of their financial emotions and the captains of their economic destinies." This is why everyone interested in understanding the wealth-building process should read this work. After reading *Who's Afraid to Be a Millionaire?* you will know how to face your financial fears and take the essential financial steps to secure the financial success you desire.

OLIVIA MELLAN
Psychotherapist and author of
Money Harmony and *The Advisor's Guide to Money Psychology*

ACKNOWLEDGMENTS

This book is the result of a four-year effort to produce the *Who's Afraid to Be a Millionaire?* television special with a companion book. It took a great deal of work, resources, time, energy, and commitment on the part of many people to sustain this multiyear project. I want to thank everyone who contributed in any way to making this project possible.

First, I must thank my co-executive producer of the *Moneywise* television show and the president of New River Media, Inc., Andrew Walworth. After attending one of my seminars Andrew got excited about producing the *Who's Afraid to Be a Millionaire?* television special. Due to his unwavering support the special along with the companion *Who's Afraid to Be a Millionaire* book were presented to the public in 2006.

Neither the television special nor the book would have been possible without my friends Cheryl McDonald of Wells Fargo Bank, and Natalie Brown and Terri Skipper of Wells Fargo Home Mortgage. Their support allowed me to present the *Who's Afraid to Be a Millionaire?* seminar to thousands of people across the country and video tape the public television special before a live audience in Washington, DC.

The public television special production turned out better than anyone could have imagined, primarily due to the efforts of our production team which included Sydney White, Kwame Alexander, Lynn Hoverman; the NRM/Team production staff; and the wonderful staff at the National Geographic Studios in Washington, DC.

I will always be grateful for being given the opportunity to collaborate on this book with the fine people from John Wiley. I must thank everyone at John Wiley from my editorial team—Debra Englander and Greg Freidman—to the promotion and production departments for their heroic effort to get this book to print in the short time we had to do it. For doing this I will always be grateful.

I was fortunate to have a great team of editors and financial professionals to help me write this book. I want to thank Allegra Bennett, Barbara O'Niell, Sabrina Parker, E. Jeanne Harnois, Diana Spencer, Dawn Converse, and Dale Berry for their editorial assistance. I am also fortunate to know experienced financial professionals who were willing to share their professional insight with me. Thank you Leon Lebreque, Carl Norris, Sidney Madlock, Mark Fisher, Reverend Floyd Flake, Rabbi Marc Israel, LeCount Davis, Luther Gatlin, Denise Murray, Marcia Griffin, John Rother, Charles Gonzales, Faye Coleman, William Keating, and Christine Fahlund.

I especially want to thank Olivia Mellan for writing the Foreword, my agent Wendy Keller, and my legal advisors, Carl Desantist and Paul Almond.

I must also thank the generous individuals who shared their stories with me and the authors who gave me permission to cite their works in this book. Finally, I need to thank all of my family members, friends, and supporters who encouraged me to complete the national speaking tour, television special, and book. These persons include Astor Boston, Arthur Money, Georgia Money, Julia Matthews, Willie Jolley, Christina Mazzanti, Adrian Harpool, Lois Vitt, Al Bundy, Audrey Bundy, Carma Ritter, Garbreille Urquhart, Diana Gregory, Sandra Friend, Carla Nelson, Keith Corbett, Janice Williams, Geraldine Hinton, Dan Perkins, Gwen Kels, and the loyal viewers of the *Moneywise* television series. I must also give honor and thanks to God for bringing all of the aforementioned resources and people together to make this book possible.

KELVIN E. BOSTON

WHO'S AFRAID TO BE A MILLIONAIRE?

Playing the Financial Success Game

Becoming wealthy is, in fact, a mind game.

—*Thomas J. Stanley*

You are one with the infinite riches of your subconscious mind. You are happy, healthy, wealthy and successful. Money flows to you freely, copiously and endlessly. You are always aware of your true self-worth. You use your talents and you are wonderfully blessed financially.

—*Joseph Murphy,* The Power of Your Subconscious Mind

It is fitting that you take a moment to consider Joseph Murphy's affirmation as you begin reading *Who's Afraid to Be a Millionaire?* because this book explains how financial anxiety may be keeping you from reaching your financial goals. It is fitting also because this book can show you how to take steps to face your financial fears and increase your net worth. Lastly, reading this book will help you understand how to better appreciate and use your financial blessings.

Many people do not realize how financially fortunate they already are, let alone how much more financially successful they can become. The harsh realities of an uncertain economy, rising unemployment, fluctuating stock markets, natural disasters, terrorism, rising interest rates, inflation, political tensions at home, and economic competition abroad can easily fill your mind with fear, anxiety, and apprehension. Such fear hinders people's ability to appreciate their financial blessings and prevents them from comprehending their future financial opportunities.

With *Who's Afraid to Be a Millionaire,* you learn how to use knowledge to understand your financial fears; take action to reduce your financial fears; and foster a belief in yourself, free enterprise, and a higher power to replace your financial fears. By establishing the link between your emotional well-being and your financial well-being, you can begin to master financial and emotional success. Once you see beyond your irrational financial fears, you will behold your future success.

At first glance, this assertion would appear to be a bold statement—until one remembers the words of best-selling author Elizabeth Gawain. She once wrote, "Fear is created not by the world around us, but in the mind, by what we think is going to happen" (Rachel Smoker, *To Touch a Wild Dolphin*, Doubleday, 2001). Even though you may agree that fear is more a by-product of your mind than of the world around you, people seldom have a rational understanding about their irrational financial fears.

To master means "to have control over." When I refer to mastering your emotional and financial success, I simply mean that you can gain control over your emotional fears and financial affairs. Having such control will help you master playing the financial success game. If you are like most people, you probably haven't realized that pursuing financial success is similar to playing a game.

The Game

I noticed this resemblance one evening when I was watching the *Who Wants to Be a Millionaire?* game show. In this popular television quiz show, contestants who successfully answer a number of challenging questions walk away with a cool cash prize of one million dollars. Like millions of television viewers, I found that the show captured my imagination. My fascination grew stronger when I realized that only a few people would ever have the opportunity to be a contestant on the show. And of those few, even fewer still would win the million-dollar grand prize. But what really held me in awe was the notion that millions of Americans were watching this game show without understanding that, in the game of life, they were contestants in a reality game that would ultimately determine their financial success.

As a financial journalist for almost 15 years, my professional curiosity filled my mind with one question. I began to wonder if pursuing financial success could be compared to playing a game. To my surprise, I realized that the answer to my question was yes.

Yes, accumulating wealth is like playing a game. In my career as a financial planner, author, and journalist, I have interviewed self-made millionaires from all walks of life. Some were factory workers and others were successful business owners. But I did not see what most of them had in common until I perceived the similarities between financial success and game playing. Most self-made millionaires, I now realized, shared a similar characteristic regardless of their income, gender, or race—they all knew how to masterfully play life's great financial game.

According to Webster's New World dictionary (Hoboken, NJ: John Wiley & Sons, 2003), a *game* is "any activity that resembles a game, for example one that involves intense interest and competitiveness and is carried out by specific and often unspoken rules." This definition would apply to the wealth-building process. When people pursue financial success, they often become intensely interested in a wealth-building strategy, asset, or tool.

Most wealth-building assets, whether they are mutual funds, real estate, or business opportunities, are governed by their own specific and unspoken economic rules. When investors purchase shares of a mutual fund, a home, or a business, they must understand the economic rules associated with such assets to enjoy the economic benefits they desire. These rules may include interest rate, market fluctuations, appreciation, or return on investment.

Additionally, people often compete with themselves when they pursue their financial goals. Maybe they want to see how fast they can make their investments grow or how soon they will be financially able to retire. But it is still a competition. Therefore, pursuing financial success fits within the definition of playing a game. It is important for everyone to understand how to successfully play the great financial game of life. (I like to refer to the wealth-building process as the "great financial game of life" because this game can affect every aspect of your life.)

Whether you decide to play this game or decline, you will still be a participant. You may choose to use your credit wisely or misuse it. Both cases will eventually affect your financial life. You may choose to become a homeowner or to become a lifelong renter of homes. Again, both choices will have a great impact on your financial life. Likewise, you may choose to regularly save in your company's 401(k) pension plan, or you may decide never to use the company's plan. Whatever course of action or inaction you decide to take will have a great impact on your financial life. Every financial decision you make or choose not to make affects your financial well-being. This is why it is important to master the financial game of life.

This point was perhaps made most clear to me after I had completed a speaking engagement at Smith College in Albany, New York. After a presentation, audience members often approach me to ask questions. Therefore, I was not surprised when a middle-aged, gray-haired gentleman approached me. What did surprise me was the comment he shared with me. "Thank you," he said. "Your presentation helped me understand that building wealth is a game. Over the years, I have been talking myself out of the game." The dazed expression on his face indicated that it was a moment of enlightenment for this person. His comment illustrates what can happen if you don't understand that building wealth is like playing a game.

To masterfully play the financial game of life means having the wherewithal to successfully obtain your dreams. This definition does not limit itself to just financial dreams. Some people rightly understand that success in life is about more than money. It is about lifestyle. It is about deciding which dreams are important to you and then making sure you have the economic means to enjoy them.

Many people desire a lifestyle that will enable them to own a home, provide their children with a quality education, allow them to travel to faraway places, and enjoy a comfortable retirement. It is hard to put an exact price tag on acquiring such a lifestyle. But we do not need to know the price of success to win the great financial game of life.

Profile in Courage

Jeffrey lives his life in such a manner because he mastered playing the financial success game early in life. With a boom box under each arm and a stack of discs at his disposal, Jeffrey had already attained his first taste of the American dream before he was even old enough to drive.

"I saved up the money, bought some gear, and built a production company, a very small production company, but at the height of it I had about six people working full-time, and I was making some pretty sweet loot," he said of the company he started while he was in sixth grade.

Now, 11 years later, the senior electrical engineering-turned-music major has earned a list of credentials that few professional, let alone collegiate, résumés could match. Jeffrey, who estimates his wealth to be near $1.1 million, is the co-owner of three businesses: the Boston Entertainment Group (an event management company); the Comedy Lounge in Cape Cod; and Fairbanks Properties, which specializes in developing state-of-the-art facilities.

His range of unique experiences is even more diverse. Jeffrey can play the saxophone and guitar; has climbed nearly 10,000 feet above sea level in the Swiss Alps; holds a third-degree black belt in two forms of martial arts; met former President Bill Clinton while he was still in office; and appeared in six episodes of MTV's Say What? Karaoke *before going on to win the program's grand championship.*

"Jeff has done more in 23 years than most people have done in their entire lives," said his business partner, John, who graduated from Northeastern University in 2004. "It's crazy. I was shocked by it all."

Soon, Jeffrey plans to add yet another accomplishment to his catalog: an undergraduate degree from Northeastern. "I want people to say, 'Look at that kid—he went to Northeastern, and look at all the stuff he did while he was still in school' because I'm totally not any better than anybody else," Jeffrey said.

Even with his undergraduate career winding down, Jeffrey still maintains a rigorous schedule. In addition to the oversight of his businesses, he is taking five courses—the extra one to compensate for switching majors—and working full-time at Sovereign Bank to learn more about finance, an interest he first developed in high school.

Learning the Game

Jeffrey can do what he loves to do because he has mastered playing the wealth-building game. Regardless of your age, *Who's Afraid to Be a Millionaire* can help you master the financial game of life. This book is divided into two parts. The three chapters in Part One focus on mastering emotional success. In Chapter 1, you learn how to understand your financial fears. You also learn how to use knowledge, action, and belief to master these fears.

In Chapter 2, you learn how to increase your intellectual capital, protect your physical capital, and embrace your spiritual capital. Chapter 3 explores how planning can help you manage your financial life. After completing Part One, you will know how to master the fears that can sabotage your efforts to successfully play the financial game of life.

The six chapters in Part Two present the processes for mastering financial success—how to control your financial resources and make use of wealth-building opportunities.

In Chapter 4, you learn how to manage your credit. In Chapter 5 you find out how to become a homeowner. Chapter 6 explains the basics of investing in stocks. Chapter 7 highlights securing your retirement. In Chapter 8, you learn methods for protecting your income, and Chapter 9 looks at how to start a business. After reading Part Two, you will understand how to master the wealth-building steps that help people win the financial game of life.

Each chapter includes an excerpt from a relevant interview with a leading financial expert, originally aired on the *Moneywise* PBS television series. I hope you will think of these interviews as a Master's Class or Seminar. When selecting these interviews, I tried to imagine the questions you might ask someone who was a master of a specific financial subject. Each *Moneywise* Master Class interview offers you useful insights about winning the financial game of life.

Each chapter ends with a list of master keys. The master keys serve as a brief review of the material covered in the chapter. The three master keys are *Know—Act—Believe*. They will remind you to use knowledge (Know) to refute your fears and understand basic wealth-building strategies. The master keys will also remind you to take action (Act) to eliminate your financial fear and implement your financial plans. Lastly, the master keys will remind you to develop a belief (Believe) in yourself, free enterprise, and a higher power that can replace your financial fear and allow you to pursue your financial dreams.

The Conclusion highlights how mastering your emotional fears and financial resources can help you become the millionaire next door.

In the Financial Success Resource Guide, you will find contact addresses, recommended books, web sites, and other helpful information for playing the financial success game.

Financial Peace

Throughout this book, case studies will introduce you to real people who are successfully playing life's wealth-building game. For privacy reasons, I only use their first names. Some are millionaires, others are millionaires in the making. Still, all of them have found the courage to face their financial fears and take control of their financial lives. To me, each of them represents a profile in financial courage.

Many people who have mastered playing life's financial game often enjoy a certain level of emotional freedom. This financial joy occurs when people cease worrying about their finances. Their personal net worth exceeds the national median ($55,000). But it is not their financial success that brings them financial peace. It is their financial peace that allows them to enjoy their financial success. You, too, can enjoy financial peace of mind.

President John F. Kennedy once said, "We cannot let our fears hold us from pursuing our hopes." With your purchase of this book, you decided that you would not let your financial fears keep you from pursuing your financial hopes. Reading *Who's Afraid to Be a Millionaire?* will show you how to master playing the great financial game of life. Armed with this knowledge, you will enjoy financial peace of mind because you will understand that you are the master of your financial fears and the captain of your financial destiny.

PART ONE

MASTERING
EMOTIONAL SUCCESS

True success is overcoming the fear of being unsuccessful.

—Paul Sweeney

Four steps to achievement: Plan purposefully, prepare prayerfully, proceed positively, pursue persistently.

—William A. Ward

If one advances confidently in the direction of his dreams, and endeavors to live the life which he has imagined, he will meet with a success unexpected in common hours.

—Henry David Thoreau

What God expects us to attempt, He also enables us to achieve.

—Stephen Olford

Wealth was originally perceived as a state of mind, not a condition of purse.

—Richard Gaylord Brilley

Worry is nothing less than the misuse of your imagination.

—Ed Foreman

To me, the model of progress is not linear. Success is completing the full circle of yourself.

—Gloria Steinem

1

UNDERSTANDING YOUR FINANCIAL FEARS

I finally know what distinguishes man from other beasts: financial worries.

—*Jules Renard*

EMOTIONAL FACTOR:
Fear of Financial Success

I am not afraid to be a millionaire!" That is what people often declare when they learn that the title of this book is *Who's Afraid to Be a Millionaire?*

While I am pleased to see the book's title spark such an enthusiastic response, I always wait to hear the person's next comment. Some people simply smile and move on looking perplexed. Others ponder the book's title for a moment and murmur softly to themselves, "I don't think I am afraid," then smile at me and move on. Everyone wants to read the book just to confirm their belief that they are not afraid to become millionaires.

This book's title compels readers to ask themselves, "Has fear been an invisible nemesis undermining my financial success?" For many Americans, the answer probably is *yes*.

Every day, Americans must cope with the economic realities of living in the twenty-first century. Our economy is totally different from the one that our parents and grandparents had to face. Most of us know it is unlikely that our employers will continue to provide insurance to pay for our medical bills when we retire. Many of us don't know how we will afford the ever-increasing costs of housing, food, and education. Likewise, we are concerned about the economic instability of the Social Security program. The bottom line is that most Americans hope to achieve the American dream their parents believed in, but the reality is that families today don't know if and how they will afford it. This financial fear creates anxiety in many American households. Sometimes the fear fades, but it lingers deep in our individual and collective psyches. You will be well served to understand financial anxieties and how to cope with them. This book can help you.

Behavioral economists, psychologists, and researchers have been studying the connection between economics and psychology for some time. At the Hebrew University in Jerusalem in the late 1960s, Amos Tversky and Daniel Kahneman started psychological experiments to determine how people make financial decisions. Their research helped in the formulation of *judgmental heuristics* that identify how people make quick financial decisions. Their studies suggest that people's personal economic decisions often are more emotionally based than rationally based. In 2002, Kahneman shared a Nobel Prize in Economics for his pioneering work. As a result of the efforts of Tversky, Kahneman, and many other researchers, we are beginning to understand the relation between our emotional life and our financial life.

Let's focus on the most recognized symbol of financial success—money. Our relationship with money is an odd affair. Money is an inanimate object that societies the world over use as their core medium of exchange for goods and services. Still humans often seem to bestow life-giving powers on money and create many powerful money myths.

Money Myths

In her ground-breaking examination of money and relationships, Olivia Mellan, author of *Money Harmony* (Walker Publishing, 1994) writes, "Most Americans believe in at least one money myth; many of us believe in a number of them." These beliefs, she continues, "can trigger intense emotions about money (anxiety, fear, obsession) and can even make it difficult for us to handle the simplest financial decisions." According to Mellan, here are the most common money myths:

Money = Freedom
Money = Happiness
Money = Love
Money = Power
Money = Security
Money = Self-worth

After reviewing this list, it is easy to understand why people have created money myths. Each myth offers a hint of truth about this innate object we call money, but it is also easy to see how these and other money myths could distort a person's understanding and relationship with money. We are fortunate to have committed financial therapists like Mellan to help us understand, "Money does not equal happiness, love, power, freedom, self-worth or security. Money equals dollars and cents." The best-selling financial author Venita VanCaspel points out that money is our servant and not the other way around. She wrote in *Money Dynamics:*

> It is important to keep money in its proper place. It is vital to your well-being, but it is only a servant, a tool. Granted that money is necessary to modern life, but you only need so much of it to live comfortably, securely, and well. Too much emphasis on money can reverse your whole life and make you the servant and money the master" (Venita VanCaspel, *Money Dynamics for the 1990s,* Simon & Schuster, 1988).

VanCaspel's reference to people's relationship to money in terms of servant and master is timely because fear can also cause people to be subservient to their financial phobias instead of overcoming them. Although money has neither life nor life-giving properties, through the ages, it has struck fear in the hearts of people.

Age of Financial Anxiety

It is natural for people to fear what they don't know or cannot understand. Kathleen Gurney, a pioneer in financial psychology and the author of *Your Money Personality: What It Is and How You Can Profit From It* (Financial Psychology Corporation, 1988), writes "Anxiety over one's finances is a condition of life. It's a constellation of uncomfortable, troubled feelings that nearly everyone has experienced in one form or another. We live in an anxiety-producing and uncertain economic environment. You would be inhuman not to feel worried, or even terrified, about money now and then."

Americans, Gurney writes, have been conditioned to worry about money; it's part of our capitalistic birthright. Money problems are an accepted part of the price we pay for living in a competitive, free enterprise society. There is, however, a big difference between money problems and money worries, and most of our thoughts fall into the latter category. Regardless of income, most people don't feel particularly good about their financial status. But worrying about money is never a solution to a money problem.

In addition to worrying about their personal financial situation, many people worry about how their financial circumstances could be devastated by a natural disaster, terrorist attack, new national economic policy, major corporate decision, or a major correction in the ever-changing financial markets.

People have good reason to worry because unexpected financial disasters occur more frequently in our lives than we acknowledge. Many people are panic stricken when they realize they are living in uncertain economic times that are made riskier by uncontrollable environmental disasters. Coping with these new stresses means that Americans must secure their financial future in a time of great financial anxiety. Understanding financial fear can help you accomplish this task.

Financial Fear

When cited in this book, financial fear refers to a feeling of discomfort, including a panic attack, that interferes with a person's ability to deal with daily financial affairs. Worrying constantly about money can undermine the quality of people's daily lives. What is it about financial fear that is so crippling? This type of fear is the ultimate head game, but no one is playing it with us. We do it to ourselves just by thinking about what we are afraid of; we don't need to be in the actual situation. The more we think about the object of our economic stress, the more we become entrenched in the status quo of our economic existence.

The fear of money, clinically named *chrematophobia,* is perhaps the most widely known financial fear. At its extreme, chrematophobia produces symptoms such as dizziness, perspiration, loss of breath, nausea, dry mouth, heart palpitations, and the inability to think clearly. We recognize these symptoms as an *anxiety attack.*

What we often fail to recognize are the different types of financially related fears that affect our monetary decisions. Because these financial fears may not be severe enough to cause even a brief panic attack, they often go undetected and are rarely treated or resolved. Still, these undetected financial fears can cause serious short-term emotional discomfort and long-term financial disease.

Short-term emotional discomfort occurs in many first-time homeowners, investors, and entrepreneurs. Most of these financial novices overcome their fears, but some do not and may suffer the emotional and economic symptoms of financial disease. They often feel as if their financial life is not all that it could be or should be.

To help you avoid that feeling, we are not limiting our discussion to just the fear of money. To help you master your financial fears, the following phobias' financial impact are considered in this book: *plutophobia,* the fear of success (both financial and personal success); *decidophobia,* the fear of making decisions; *hypengyophobia,* the fear of taking responsibility; *metathesiophobia,* the fear of change; *chrematophobia,* the fear of money (financial loss); *gerascophobia,* the fear of growing older; *thantophobia,* the fear of discussing mortality; *atychiphobia,* fear of failure; and *orthophobia,* the fear of owning property. This list of financial fears seems straightforward and easy to grasp. But what is neither straightforward nor easy to grasp is how these fears can impact your monetary life.

Each of the aforementioned financial fears can be directly connected to one of the financial success strategies described in this book. Studying

Table 1.1
Emotional Factor Chart

Financial Fear Factors	*Financial Success Strategies*
Fear of financial success	Becoming a millionaire
Fear of personal success	Developing human capital
Fear of making financial decisions	Financial planning
Fear of taking financial responsibility	Managing credit
Fear of changing comfort zone	Becoming a homeowner
Fear of losing money	Investing in stocks
Fear of growing older	Saving for retirement
Fear of discussing mortality	Insuring your financial dreams
Fear of business failure	Starting a business
Fear of owning property	Becoming the millionaire next door

Table 1.1 will help you understand how various financial fears can impact various financial goals.

Where to Get Help

The goal of this book is to help more people understand their financial fears. Still, it must be stated that the information presented here does not represent or purport to represent medical or financial advice. For such information, you should seek counsel from a medical or financial professional. Always seek professional advice before you take any action that will impact your emotional or financial well-being.

Most people can cope with the minor financial worries they encounter every day when making economic decisions. However, severe cases of financial fears may require professional assistance. Persistent financial anxieties and other social anxiety disorders are treated by a wide variety of health professionals, including psychiatrists, psychologists, clinical social workers, and psychiatric nurses. In the United States, anxiety disorders are the most commonly diagnosed mental condition in adults between the ages of 18 and 54 years. Each year, the cost of treatment exceeds $42 billion (1993 study from the Institute for Behavior and Health in Rockville, MD). Anxiety disorders are no laughing matter, especially because many trigger symptoms of physical illness.

This book can help readers better understand the link between financial fear and the wealth-building process. At the same time, it may help readers who have suffered much from persistent financial fears realize that they need to seek professional help. I encourage readers to seek professional advice if their financial phobias severely disrupt their daily life.

You can learn more about anxiety disorders by contacting the Anxiety Disorders Association of America (ADAA) in Silver Spring, Maryland, at www.adaa.org. The ADAA provides educational materials, a quarterly newsletter, and state-by-state listings of self-help groups and mental health professionals who specialize in treating anxiety disorders.

The Three Master Keys

Studying, understanding, and implementing the three master keys presented in this book will enhance your emotional and financial well-being. Sections that focus on the three master keys—Knowledge, Action, and Belief—appear at the end of each chapter.

To master your economic anxiety, for example, you can find guidance in knowledge to refute the irrational foundation of your fear. Under Action, you learn how to move beyond your fear to Belief. You must learn to believe in yourself, free enterprise, and a higher power that can replace your fear. As explained in this chapter, these master keys can help you understand, implement, and believe in your ability to reach your financial goals.

Knowledge

There are three ways we can use knowledge to help us play the money game. First, we can gain confidence by increasing our general knowledge about financial fear and financial wealth-building strategies. You should think of your financial education as an enjoyable lifelong learning process. We cover the subject of knowledge in detail when we review enhancing your intellectual capital in Chapter 2. For now, I just want to point out that you should never underestimate the wealth-creating power of financial knowledge.

Second, you can use knowledge to master the money game by learning the acronym I have created for the word *fear*. In my acronym, the letters FEAR stand for "False Economic Anxieties Appearing Real." That is what fear means to people who have learned how to play the wealth-building game.

One of the realities about financial fear is that much of what frightens us is not real. We perceive things as we think they are or as we think they will turn out. How many times have you worried yourself sick over a financial situation only to discover that it wasn't as bad as you thought after all? We cannot read the financial future, yet we worry about it often, creating a horror show in our minds. Remembering the acronym FEAR will help you to stop creating financial horror shows in your mind.

Third, you can use your knowledge of financial fear-reduction strategies to avoid the traps created by your economic anxieties. Just knowing these strategies will help you avoid many of these emotional traps. Financial fear-reduction strategies are listed in Table 1.2. Throughout this book, I describe steps you can take to limit the economic havoc that financial fear can inflict on your financial life.

Table 1.2
Financial Fear-Reduction Strategies

Fear Factors	Fear-Reduction Strategies
Fear of financial success	Learn more about the wealth-building process
Fear of personal success	Embrace success with your body, mind, and spirit
Fear of making decisions	Implement the strategies in your financial plan
Fear of financial responsibility	Take responsibility for your financial life
Fear of changing comfort zone	Move beyond your physical comfort zone
Fear of losing money	Start investing monthly in a mutual fund
Fear of growing older	Plan and save for your dream retirement
Fear of discussing mortality	Enjoy planning and sharing your good fortune (or insurance) with others
Fear of business failure	Start a part-time home-based business
Fear of owning property	Invest in more appreciating assets

Knowing financial fear reduction strategies will help you avoid or escape many emotional traps. One of my favorite sayings is, "If knowledge does represent power, then financial knowledge must represent financial power." This being the case, the information that you glean from the Knowledge master key sections will empower you emotionally and financially.

Action

The second master key—Action—may be the most important one because it can help you face your financial fears. The ultimate way to reduce fear is to act on it. Eleanor Roosevelt offered similar advice. She observed, "You gain strength, courage, and confidence by every experience in which you really stop to look fear in the face. . . . You must do the thing you think you cannot do" (John Cook, *The Book of Positive Quotations,* Rubicon Press, 1993).

One of my acquaintances didn't have a choice. He was forced to face his financial fear. Robert was afraid of the whole financial thing. Being single, he is solely responsible for his own keep. He said that he used to be afraid of the financial upheaval if he should lose his job and not be able to pay his rent.

He has family and friends, so it is unlikely he would ever have ended up on the street collecting soda cans, but he still had been fearful. He feared losing his independence and his lifestyle. But he is not afraid of this anymore.

Why? Because his fear was realized when he did lose his job. He went through a bleak time, and guess what? He survived. He is no longer afraid of what might happen, because now he knows that he has the fortitude to see himself through if he again loses his job or faces some other financial crisis.

Robert overcame his fear of job loss after he was forced to deal with losing a job. I hope that you will not be forced to face your fears. Nevertheless, to overcome your fear, you will eventually have to face it. Where financial fear is concerned, you should seriously consider the advice offered in the Nike advertisements and "Just Do It!" The second master key—Action—will remind you to just do it. Take action and face your financial fear.

Face Your Fears

One of the most effective ways to face your fears is to write them down. You can do this on your computer or with pen and notepad. Just begin writing down your financial fears. Don't edit as you go along. Allow the thoughts to stream out of your mind. . . . No matter how small the financial concern is, write it down. When completed, your list may include everything from paying a credit card bill to the inevitable breakup with your significant other. Your list may also include your concerns about the stock market and the state of a military conflict in another land. Whatever causes you any financial anguish, put it on your list. Once you write down your financial fears, you will begin to see how you can effectively address them.

When undertaken sincerely, this exercise is amazingly utilitarian, and a surprising shift is bound to occur in your thinking, from helpless, overwhelmed mind to strategic mind. This is the most dynamic aspect of writing the list and thus has great potential for personal growth.

Once you have made your list, look it over and put an "R" next to the items that seem real to you and an "F" next to the ones that, with a little thought, you see are false fears. Once done, spend a little more time looking at each item you have marked with an R. These are the money fears you believe are beyond your control. Perhaps that R item is a tax problem or several overwhelming loans heading toward default.

After you have reviewed your list of identified fears, it is time to take action. If there is an item on your list that you can do something about, such as reducing your credit card usage, take the steps to do so. Some items on your list may require assistance or professional help for resolution. In that case, by all possible means, seek professional help. If necessary, talk to a financial counselor, financial planner, or mental health professional.

Lastly, if there are fears on your list that you can't do anything about— the state of the economy or a terrorist attack or a natural disaster—turn those concerns over to a higher power and get on with your life. I once saw a small poster that read, "Every evening I turn my worries over to God. He is going to be up all night anyway" (Mary C. Crowley). It is a wonderful reminder to set aside your financial worries at the end of the day. If you have acted on those financial matters that you can act on and found help for those that require help, then why shouldn't you let go and let a higher source handle those financial concerns that are beyond your control? People who have placed their financial concerns on paper say this simple exercise helps take loads of pressure off their minds and hearts.

Know Your Financial Comfort Zone

In addition to helping you face your financial fears, taking action will help you move beyond your financial comfort zone and overcome secondhand financial stress that prevents you from achieving emotional and financial success.

Rhonda Britten, career coach and author of *Fearless Living* (Berkley Publishing, 2001), conducts seminars across the country to help people live without fear. In *Fearless Living,* she writes, "Fear is the gatekeeper of your comfort zone" (p. 23). Your comfort zone is whatever is familiar to you. Your financial comfort zone would represent those financial experiences and matters with which you are familiar. All other financial experiences and concerns could make you feel apprehensive. Why? Because these new or seemingly risky financial situations would not be a part of your normal financial comfort zone.

None of us can choose the time when personal financial opportunities will come our way. But we must be emotionally prepared to seize such moments when they occur. Being emotionally prepared means sensibly understanding the fortunate circumstance, evaluating the risk, and confidently taking action to benefit from the event. Too many people let financial opportunities pass them by because their fear has paralyzed them and they cannot get beyond their financial comfort zones.

Overcome Secondhand Financial Stress

Financial fear originates from many sources. In some ways, it comes from living in a free enterprise society, as Gurney suggests. From time to time, the news media, political leaders, and CEOs (chief executive officers) of major corporations have frightened the American public with dire economic, financial, and business news. But people may exhibit the more extreme symptoms of financial fear after being exposed to the fears of friends, coworkers, and even family members. Passing fear from one person to another person has been referred to as *transference,* or what I like to call *secondhand financial stress.* Like secondhand smoke, such fears can be hazardous to your physical health. Secondhand financial stress can also be hazardous to your emotional and financial health. I know firsthand, because like so many others, I had to learn how to overcome secondhand financial stress.

Case Study

I was in my late 30s when I realized that my mother's financial comfort zone was in some ways still shaping my own. I didn't discover that my mother harbored a fear of being self-employed until I decided to become self-employed. Many years ago when I decided to start my business, the first person I called to tell the good news was my mother. I was so excited. When my mother answered the phone, I said, "Mama, I am going to own my own business."

I expected to hear my mother's excitement on the other end of the phone. But all I heard was a long loud silence. Then my mother said, "Boy, why are you going to waste that good education? You're not a businessman."

Then my mother's fear kicked in, and she roused the alarm. "Boy, you don't know anything about business. You have never owned a business, and you don't have no business going into business." That was the essence of my mother's advice and support at the time.

I still started my business, but from time to time, I would remember my mother's discouraging words. There were times when I thought that my mother was right. I lost a lot of money the first few years that I was self-employed. During those early years of my entrepreneurial career, I had a lot of nightmares in which my mama would be chasing me around the house demanding back the money she gave me for my college education. While chasing me, she would shout, "You're not a businessman. You're not a businessman."

It took some time for me to realize that my mother's doubts were contributing to my business progress or, more correctly, my lack of business progress.

My mother had unknowingly passed her fears to me. Once I began to understand what was happening, I started to confront the fear of business ownership that my mother had instilled in me. It took a lot of time and effort, but eventually I turned my business around.

After a few years of positive business growth, an interesting thing happened. On my mother's birthday, I was so busy working that I did not have time to buy her a gift. So I just sent her a check. After receiving the check in the mail, my mother called me, and over the phone she said, "Baby, you're such a *gooood* businessman!"

Needless to say, it was one of the best telephone calls that I have ever gotten in my life. But that call from my mother came almost a decade after she had contaminated my business dreams with her fear. Today, I am glad that I pursued my entrepreneurial dreams despite her doubts. I hate to even think about what career path I would have taken had my mother's fear kept me from pursuing my dreams.

It took me a while to understand how my mother's fear had shaped my own. But once I realized that my mother had passed along her fear of being self-employed to me, I could correct it.

Once you identify the origin of your money attitudes and opinions, then you can adjust them. Because fears often spread from one family member to another, your financial fears may come from your family roots. The fear you inherit from a family member may be the longest lasting and hardest to overcome. Simple discussions around the family dinner table can mark our attitudes about money, investing, and success for better or worse through-out our lives.

Case Study

Grace, a graphic artist, comes right out and says it: "I was brought up believing money was evil. Not bad, but evil. I'm intellectually over it, but right now I am in personal financial trouble and don't know how to begin to get out." Grace may be intellectually over the bad slogans, but she nonetheless is rooted in them, stuck in the fear. When offered advice on how to sort out her financial problem, she frowned at a suggestion that she personally gather her bills and write them down on paper. She resisted, arguing that her situation can be solved only by the professional attention of an accountant, and she quickly added, "I can't afford to hire that kind of service." So she remains rigidly in her financially stressed comfort zone.

While she is still working to improve her money management skills, Grace must be given credit for deciding that she no longer wants her financial life to be governed by the financial values of her parents.

Like Grace, you may realize that your attitudes about money were established in your formative years. As children, we hear adults matter-of-factly reinforcing each other's negative view of financial success. As we grow, it becomes part of the oral traditions that are fed to us and that we internalize and pass along.

Around the dinner table, we listen as the adults curse wealth or denounce its absence in their lives. We hear them repeatedly condemn the "mean green" as the "root of all evil" and reference the Bible to support this view. "It must be true, it was in the Bible."

They declare that "money doesn't buy happiness," "it doesn't grow on trees," and "I'll never have enough." They say, "I'll end up in the poorhouse," and a string of other self-defeating, ultimately self-fulfilling prophecies. As a consequence, from one generation to the next, we pass on these beliefs as a kind of oral history. We adopt and transfer feelings of guilt for wanting "too much money." We righteously declare that money is unimportant in our lives and that we only need to "earn just enough to make it in this world."

Not surprisingly, these are self-fulfilling words. Most of our lives, we make just enough to barely make it, remain frustrated for more, and are clueless that the dearth of wealth in our lives is in direct response to the belief system we have been cultivating all along.

Florence Scovel Shinn was a gifted twentieth-century metaphysician and writer whose work was published between 1925 and 1945. In one of her enduring books, *The Game of Life and How to Play It* (Simon & Schuster, 1925), she wrote, "No man can attract money if he despises it. Many people are kept in poverty by saying: 'Money means nothing to me and I have contempt for people who have it.'" Expressing contempt for financial success is the very attitude that separates us from it. Such boastfulness might have been designed to exhibit financial virtues, but it also exposes financial fear.

Parental displays of financial angst can foster fear in children. More parental care is advised in this matter. Often just a better choice of words can help children develop positive money attitudes along with a stronger sense of financial security.

Diana was fortunate that her father instilled in her frugality tempered with reason.

Millionaire in the Making

Diana, 49, works with a Certified Public Accountant and has been planning for success for more than 20 years. She has investments in stocks and in real estate, but right now, she says that real estate is her most productive investment. She says that living a frugal lifestyle has actually led her to live a better lifestyle.

She began her retirement savings when she started her career at age 21, and she got into real estate in her early 30s after deciding to generate some additional income. She now owns her own home and three other investment properties.

She attributes her lifelong patterns of saving and spending wisely to ingrained behaviors from her childhood. Diana's father heavily influenced her spending habits. He taught his six children at an early age to save. They also watched how he lived.

He was, by Diana's account, a thrifty person and showed his children how to live a frugal—and financially rewarding—lifestyle. She says, "I didn't grow up in an affluent home. I wasn't given everything on a silver platter, so I have an appreciation for what I earn."

Enrolling in a 401(k) when she first started working 28 years ago has allowed her to appreciate the compound interest theory, as she is already seeing the result of years of accumulation. Saving with a 401(k) has never been a hardship for her; as she says, "What you don't see, you don't miss." She also is careful with her annual and other performance bonuses. She is never tempted to take the money and splurge, instead, she either adds it to her investment portfolio or uses it to pay down a mortgage, increasing her equity.

She knows she is doing all the right things with her savings and 401(k). She also has a reliable pension plan, thanks to her many years with a secure company. By the time she is ready to retire, she will have fully paid for her retirement home. Her home, investments, and savings now provide her with a financial security that she describes as being able to "do what you want without having to live paycheck to paycheck." Diana's inherited money management skill seems to be serving her well. She grew up in a household that inspired her to lead a frugal but financial rewarding life. Unfortunately, not all households instill these emotional and financial attitudes in their children.

Author Olivia Mellan writes, "Most of the time, direct and open communication about a family's finances just doesn't happen. What does get communicated is free-floating anxiety, fear, and general sense of malaise. This causes a lot of psychic harm and can lead to anxiety" (*Money Harmony*, Walker Publishing, 1994, p. 38).

The point is that the financial fear you have today may have been unknowingly instilled in you when you were a child. Over the years, your parents' financial insecurities and personal circumstances, good or bad, may have nurtured your fears. Knowing the source of your fears will help you understand your comfort zone.

Your parents' fears may lead you to live in a financial comfort zone today that resembles their zone in past years. You may choose not to let your parents' financial comfort zone define your own. Financial maturity occurs when you decide to create your own comfort zone.

Once you understand the attitudes and opinions that helped shape your financial zone, then you can adjust them. The good news is that knowing you can create or re-create your comfort zone will help you successfully control your emotional and financial life.

Bob and his wife, Tracey, completely changed their financial comfort zone, and they are glad that they did. When asked how they feel about money—in fact, if they fear money—they both responded in gleeful unison, "Not anymore."

Case Study

At 39 and 40 years old, respectively, this husband and wife have become savvy and comfortable talking about and handling money. It was not always that way. "We were terrified about finances. Our fear was based on the uncertainty of its presence in our lives, that money could be cut off," Bob said. "We were taught at home to get a job, get an education, get stuff, and retire."

Both Bob and Tracey's parents worked until retirement age in jobs at the post office and at Bethlehem Steel—a big private corporation in the Baltimore, Maryland, area that employed generations of workers. The children learned that the social order of things was to get a "permanent" job working for a manufacturing company like Beth Steel or, better yet, with the federal government. For those who were diligent, a government job would mean pre-

dictable promotions with good salaries that allowed for the acquisition of a house, cars, college education for the kids, and other symbols of success. Then there was the afterlife of retirement on a good pension and medical benefits.

It was a mentality that Bob and Tracey's parents inherited from their depression-era parents and were passing along to their children. A good government job was prestigious and for decades meant lifetime employment. "But the chessboard has changed," Bob noted. Bethlehem Steel is gone, as are other huge companies that were lifetime employers. Government employment is no longer a certainty. "We can't do what our parents did."

Bob and Tracey realized they had to do something different. They were living in a new world order, and something was blocking them from making the income they wanted and having enough of what they made left at the end of the month. The couple set about uncovering the origins of their monetary view of life and mapping a strategy that would work for them the way government employment had worked for their parents.

They developed a new money philosophy. "You've got to have income working for you, not you working for income," Bob said. Seeing their financial selves on paper made them begin to think about money in a different way. "Once you begin to understand what it takes to obtain wealth, then the fear subsides and confidence takes over," Bob said.

Bob and Tracey's financial fears began to disappear once they decided to face them. Their decision to act helped them move beyond their emotional comfort zone and overcome the secondhand financial stress their parents had given to them. If you want to successfully walk the same path as Bob and Tracey, you will have to take action that can help you face your financial fears, move beyond your emotional comfort zone, and overcome secondhand financial stress. Action—the second master key—will remind you to *just do it.*

Money Autobiography Questionnaire

To identify the attitudes that helped shape your financial comfort zone, take the Money Autobiography Questionnaire (Form 1.1) developed by

Form 1.1
Money Autobiography Questionnaire

This questionnaire is designed to help you understand your relationship with money by developing an awareness of yourself in the context of culture, family, value systems, and experience. This is a process of self-discovery. To fully benefit from this exploration, please write down your answers. You will not get the full value from the exercise if you just breeze through and give mental answers. While it is recommended that you first answer these questions by yourself, many people relate that they have enjoyed sharing them with others.

As you answer these questions, be conscious of your feelings. Describe them in writing as part of your process.

1. Childhood
   a. What is your first memory of money?
   b. What was your happiest moment with money?
   c. Your unhappiest?
   d. Name the miscellaneous money messages you received as a child.
   e. How were you confronted with the knowledge of differing economic circumstances among people—that there were people "richer" than you and people "poorer" than you?
2. Cultural Heritage
   a. What is your cultural heritage, and how has your heritage traditionally interfaced with money?
   b. To the best of your knowledge, how has your heritage been impacted by the money forces? Be specific.
   c. Does this circumstance of heritage or culture have any motive related to money?
   d. Speculate about the manner in which your forebears' money handling decisions continue to affect you today.
3. Family
   a. How is/was the subject of money addressed by your church or the religious traditions of your forebears?
   b. What happened to your parents or grandparents during the Depression?
   c. How did your family communicate about money? Be as specific as you can be, but remember that we are more concerned about the impact on you than on historical veracity.
   d. When did your family immigrate to America (or its current location)? What else do you know about your family's economic circumstances historically?
4. Your Parents
   a. How did your mother address money issues?
   b. Your father?
   c. How did they differ in their attitudes toward money?
   d. How did they address money issues in their relationship?
   e. Did they argue or maintain strict silence?
   f. How do you feel about that today?
5. Please do your best to answer the same questions regarding your life or business partner(s) and their parents.

Form 1.1 *(Continued)*

6. Childhood Revisited
   a. How did you relate to money as a child? Did you feel "poor" or "rich"? Relatively?
   b. Or completely? Why? Were you anxious about money?
   c. Did you receive an allowance? If so, describe amounts and responsibilities.
      i. Did you have household responsibilities?
      ii. Did you get paid regardless of performance?
      iii. Did you work for money?
   d. If not, please describe your thoughts and feelings about that. Same questions, as a teenager, young adult, and older adult.

7. Credit
   a. When did you first acquire something on credit?
   b. When did you first acquire a credit card?
   c. What did it represent to you when you first held the credit card?
   d. Describe your feelings about credit.
   e. Do you have trouble living within your means?
   f. Do you have debt?

8. Adulthood
   a. Have your attitudes shifted during your adult life? Describe.
   b. Why did you choose your personal path?
   c. Would you do it again?
   d. Describe your feelings about credit.

9. Adult Attitudes
   a. Are you money motivated?
   b. If so, please explain why? If not, why not?
   c. How do you feel about your present financial situation?
   d. Are you financially fearful or resentful? How do you feel about that?
   e. Will you inherit money? How does that make you feel?
   f. If you feel well off today, how do you feel about the money situation of others?
   g. If you feel poor, same question.
   h. How do you feel about begging? Welfare?
   i. If you are well-off today, why are you working?
   j. Do you worry about your financial future?
   k. Are you generous or stingy? Do you treat? Do you tip?
   l. Do you give more than you receive or the reverse? Would others agree?
   m. Could you ask a close relative for a business loan? For rent/grocery money?
   n. Could you subsidize a nonrelated friend? How would you feel if that friend bought something you deemed frivolous?
   o. Do you judge others by how you perceive them dealing with their money?
   p. Do you feel guilty about your prosperity?
   q. Are your siblings prosperous?
   r. What part does money play in your spiritual life?
   s. Do you "live" your money values?

Source: "Financial Planning Handbook for Physicians and Advisory," Jones and Barlett Publishers, 2005.

David E. Marcinko, the CEO of the Institute of Medical Business Advisors, Inc., and author of the *Financial Planning Handbook for Physicians and Advisors* (Jones and Barlett Publishers, 2005).

Other questions that would be useful to answer may occur to you as you progress in your life's journey. The goal is to know your personal monetary attitudes and their ramifications for your life, work, and personal mission.

This exercise is a "work in progress" with answers both complex and incomplete.

Don't worry. Just incorporate fine-tuning your knowledge of your monetary attitudes into your daily life.

Belief

The third master key is Belief. Developing a positive belief in your self, free enterprise, and a higher power will help you replace your negative financial emotion with a positive financial emotion. This process can help you win the wealth-building game.

The Sanskrit word for faith is *visus,* which literally translated means "to have trust, to breathe freely, to be without fear." When you believe in yourself, you can trust your monetary decisions more than you trust your financial fears. When you believe in the American free enterprise system, you will breathe more freely or feel less anxious about making long-term financial decisions. When you believe in a higher power (God, Nature, Supreme Being), you will live with your financial decisions without financial fear. For these reasons, you need to constantly nurture your belief in yourself, free enterprise, and a higher power.

Belief—the third master key—will help you win the financial success game. You need to believe in yourself because gaining financial success requires courage. You will have to make many courageous economic decisions about everything, from when to pay your debts to when to invest in the stock market. While the wealth-building information in this book can help you, ultimately you must make these decisions; and for this, you will need courage. To foster your courage, always learn as much as you can about the financial matter that concerns you. You do not have to become an expert. But you can become an informed user of financial products and services. Read as much as you can about the matter under consideration. Then seek to support your findings by getting the best advice you can find about the subject at hand. After doing this research, you will be able to trust your

ability to make a positive, calculated decision. The more times you successfully use this financial decision-making process, the more you will believe
in yourself.

It is easy to live in the American free enterprise system and still not believe in it. Those of us who live in the United States tend to forget that this
nation is about the creation of wealth. Is our economic system perfect? No.
However, it still stands as the best in the world. Each day, this great society—this economic democracy—offers you many wealth-creation opportunities (home ownership, stock ownership, business ownership, employment,
education, etc.).

Each day, you must decide whether you will use these avenues to increase your net worth. That is the wonderful thing about this country. You
can access the wealth creation opportunity in the United States, or you can
choose not to do so. Let me suggest that you choose to do so. Let me also
suggest that you not take the economic incentives of living in this nation for
granted. For "only in American," to use the words of successful fight promoter Don King, can anyone become the millionaire next door. Our free
enterprise system offers you the possibility to become that millionaire. To
succeed in this system, however, you must first believe in it. Belief—the
third master key—will remind you to believe in the free enterprise system.

Your belief in a higher power can also diminish your financial fears and
therefore help you master the great financial game of life. Spiritual activities,
whether they are part of an organized spiritual group or an individualized belief in a higher power can shift the dynamics of financial fear. Herbert
Benson a renowned researcher, speculated, "Spiritual experience serves as a
physical balm to counter the rapid pulse and adrenaline rush associated with
stress." Believing in a higher power (God, Nature, Supreme Being) will help
you face your financial fear because fear and faith in a higher power cannot
occupy the same emotional space. One will eventually block out the other.
Use your belief and faith in a higher power to block your emotional and faith-
less fears. Here are a few ideas that will benefit you as you foster your belief:

- "If you begin with prayer, you will think more clearly and make fewer
  mistakes" notes the founder of the Templeton Mutual Funds, Sir John
  Marks Templeton.
- There is no lack in the universe and if you tap into the universe there
  will be no lack in what you can achieve (Catherine Ponder).

- Trust the abundant spiritual force that is always with you and wants you to succeed (Willie Jolley).
- "Every evening I turn my worries over to God," Mary C. Crowley explains, "He's going to be up all night anyway."
- Economically successful people use their strong religious faith to reduce their financial fears (Thomas Stanley).

Lastly, you should know that it will be your belief in a higher power that will give you the emotional strength to get up after your financial fear has knocked you down. Fear is something that will stay with you most of your adult life. There will be days when you will feel certain that you have overcome all financial fears, only to wake up one morning full of emotional dread about some unexpected financial problem. So while you confidently make your financial decisions, accept that financial fears will always be with you, and sometimes they may get the best of you. Sometimes your fears are going to push you down emotionally, and you may get so emotionally tired of dealing with them that you are going to just fall down.

Every time a financial fear knocks you down, you must get right back up. Remember that your financial success will not be determined by how many times your fears knock you down, but by how many times you get back up. If you stay down, your financial fears will win the emotional fight. Likewise when you get back up, you will be the winner. When your financial fears have made you fall down, use your belief in a higher power to help you get back up.

Each master key can help you play the millionaire game, but the three keys can unlock much greater emotional and financial success when you use them together. The success you want to find is not something that is outside you; it is buried deep within you. It will take knowledge, action, and belief to unlock this hidden source of success. As you continue to read this book, remember that the three master keys in each chapter are there to help you unlock your buried treasure.

Profile in Courage

Knowing that most wealthy Americans didn't inherit their wealth underscores a point often made by Gail Perry-Mason, a best-selling author, financial ad-

visor, and friend. When someone asks Perry-Mason, "How do people become financially successful?" her response is always the same: "Oftentimes, it's not your net worth, but your self-worth that determines your success."

Your self-worth represents the potential for success that is locked away within you. Gail Perry-Mason can speak about this self-worth because over the years, she has used the three master keys (Knowledge, Action, and Belief) to unlock her success.

Perry-Mason has faced numerous personal and financial challenges during her 20 years in the financial services industry. Some of them had a direct influence on her financial life, causing her many worrisome nights. But she coped effectively with all of them because she used her knowledge, took action, and kept her faith.

Twenty years ago, Gail was not a woman with a plan. She was a student, studying biology, when, as she puts it, "I had a child, got married, and was divorced all in the same year." But it was in fulfilling her immediate need to support herself and her new baby that the door to her future opened. And once she stumbled on her dream, she kept at it, reached out to those who could help her, and refused to listen to those who said no. And today she is a vice president for a major investment advisory firm.

Twenty years ago, Gail took the only job that she was qualified for, as a receptionist for a local brokerage firm. Curious and interested in people, Gail would engage the clients who came into the office in conversation. She remembers one client in particular, a woman who came in with one million dollars that she had obtained in a divorce agreement. The client's plan was to invest the windfall and live off the interest. Gail, herself recently divorced, but with a meager financial settlement, became intrigued by this woman's position. So she decided that she wanted to learn more about the investment business.

Soon thereafter, she became a secretary. In this position, she was more involved with the clients and therefore was in a better position to learn the ins and outs of the brokerage business. She decided that she wanted to study for the Series 7 test to become a broker. Her bosses discouraged her, saying that it was too difficult. (She was an exceptionally good secretary, and they preferred to keep it that way.) Gail was disheartened until one evening when she came across a Series 7 study guide that someone had left in a conference room. She leafed through the book and knew it was something she could, in fact, handle. "They told me I couldn't study for it, but when I saw the book, I knew I could do it," she said. So she zeroxed the book and studied on her own time. Unbeknownst to her bosses, she took the test and passed. When she let them know, they said that they wished she hadn't done it; but since she did, she was promoted and allowed to develop her own client base.

Gail took the same approach each step of the way throughout her career. Whenever she heard "no," she dug her heels in and kept after her goal, even if it meant finding another, nontraditional, way to achieve it. She overcame her fears with persistence and determination, keeping her eyes on her goals and remaining focused on what she wanted to achieve. "When people said, 'no,' I just did it anyway," she says.

"So many times I didn't think I could do it," Gail says, remembering those early days, when she was working two jobs (she was also a waitress), going to school (she switched to business), and raising her son, "Prayer helped, and something inside said that I had to press on."

Gail's action helped to increase her earnings over time. Every time she got a promotion (and she got many), she saw her income and net worth increase. You can do the same thing by increasing your education. Table 1.3 illustrates that progression. But it also illustrates another important point: You are probably already a millionaire in the making—a person whose life-

Table 1.3
Expected Lifetime Earnings per Educational Level

Highest Educational Attainment	Lifetime Earnings ($)
Some high school, no diploma	1,000,000
High school diploma or equivalent	1,200,000
Some college, no degree	1,500,000
Associate degree	1,600,000
Bachelor's degree	2,100,000
Master's degree	2,500,000
Doctoral degree	3,400,000
Professional degree	4,400,000

Source: "The Big Payoff: Educational Attainment and Estimates of Work-Life Earnings," U.S. Census Bureau, 2000.

time earnings will surpass a million dollars. Now that is the good news. The bad news is that you could still end up flat broke when you are ready to retire if you do not make proper use of your financial resources. To avoid this misfortune, successfully deploy your emotional energies and financial resources. While you are reading this book, always remember that you are a "millionaire in the making" with the emotional capacity and the financial wherewithal to win the millionaire game.

Moneywise Master Class

When Mark Fisher, author of *The Instant Millionaire* (New World Library, 1990), was my guest on the *Moneywise* television series, he shared several tips that all millionaires in the making will find useful. Here is a portion of my interview with Fisher:

BOSTON: Mark, in your book, *The Instant Millionaire,* you talk about attitude and having a million-dollar consciousness. How can people develop a million-dollar attitude?

FISHER: You must be aware of the fact that you're worth more than you or others might think. For example, the other day I was giving a speech and a lady came to me and said "Mr. Fisher, Mr. Fisher, I'm very excited. Last week I was going for an interview. I said to myself that I wasn't going to take anything under $25,000 a year. And the night before my interview I read your book, and I said why not ask $40,000?" And she asked for it, and she got it. I said, "Not too bad for a two-hour read, you know a $15,000 raise." So just the fact of being aware that maybe you're worth more than you think, will help you begin the process.

BOSTON: What can people do so that they can prepare themselves to become financially secure?

FISHER: Read books because it expands your consciousness. Sometimes, you just get one thing in a book that is going to help you get to another level or just give you another idea that's going to bring you great success.

BOSTON: Anything else?

FISHER: People have to take action. It's one thing to read a very good book, but you must take action on what you read.

BOSTON: You have written that people pursuing success must be fearless. Why?

FISHER: If you don't believe in yourself, you're not going to take action. And the first time you see failure you're going to stop. I read a lot of books about very successful people. They have a lot of failure but they try again and they finally make it.

BOSTON: If I'm an ordinary, average hard-working individual, can I become a millionaire?

FISHER: You have to be a believer. You have to be a dreamer, and you have to take action. And stick to it. A lot of people quit early. My seventh book was successful. My six previous books didn't do well. People have asked me, "Why did you keep on writing?" I said, "because I thought I would make it eventually." Sometimes it takes time and you have to persevere.

The title of this book raises this question to readers: *Who's Afraid to Be a Millionaire?* The answer is, all readers who:

- Have not faced their financial fears
- Have not moved beyond their financial comfort zone
- Have not overcome secondhand stress
- Have not learned to use knowledge, action, and belief to control their emotional and financial well-being

Now take a moment to review the master keys for this chapter.

MASTER KEYS

Know

If you want to conquer fear, don't sit at home and think about it. Go out and get busy.

—*Dale Carnegie*

Act

Understand your financial comfort zone.
Write your financial autobiography.
Know that fear is a false economic anxiety that appears to be real.
Make a list of your fears.
When fear knocks you down, always get back up.
Use knowledge, action, and belief to control your emotional and financial success.

Believe

I am not afraid to become a millionaire!
I am a millionaire in the making!

2

DEVELOPING YOUR HUMAN CAPITAL

If only God would give me a sign like depositing a large sum of money in my bank account.

—Woody Allen

EMOTIONAL FACTOR:
Fear of Personal Success

Fear of personal success is a beguiling anxiety. At one point or another in our lives, most of us have had to deal with our fear of personal success. Yet, few of us will ever admit it. This is the fear that causes you not to apply for that promotion at work, even when you know that you are the best candidate for the job. The same fear causes you to say no to that great opportunity when you know deep down inside, you should say yes to it. And the same fear forces you to stay in a tedious comfort zone, instead of embracing the joy-filled life you truly desire.

Fear of personal success is the reason many people's economic earnings seem to plateau at a certain level. It is not because they want that to happen or because they have no other options. It is because they are afraid to take on the new responsibilities, a new lifestyle, and yes, the new opportunities that might come with success.

One of the great privileges of living in the United States is that we all can define success on our own terms. One of the great ironies of living in this nation is that we also have the right to enjoy financial stagnation on our own terms.

One of the best ways to counteract the negative influences caused by fear is to embrace what you fear—in this case, success. In this chapter, you will learn how to use your physical, mental, and spiritual capital to increase your financial net worth. Furthermore, you will discover that success is about more than money and that indeed God wants you to be successful. Lastly, you will come to understand the connection between developing your human capital and overcoming your fear of personal success.

An important aspect of playing the wealth-building game that often is taken for granted or totally overlooked is *human capital*—your potential to learn, work, and produce needed income for your family. Cheryl has never taken her human capital for granted. She knows how to increase her intellectual capital, protect her physical capital, and embrace her spiritual capital.

Profile in Courage

Cheryl is a 43-year-old bond trader who lives in New York City. When Cheryl was in her late teens, she intuitively constructed a philosophy about handling her money, creating objectives, and developing a plan of execution. She wanted a life of wealth and comfort and defined it as one that included annual vacations to great destinations, the ability to go to nice places around town with her friends, and enough income to enjoy fun things at will, without worrying about whether she could afford them.

What's more, a life of wealth and comfort would mean she would be utterly comfortable with all her basics taken care of along with some luxury.

Finally, "There would be no angry letters from anyone"; her future, in short, would be secure.

Cheryl was in her early 20s when she started playing the wealth-building game. She bought her first property at age 23, a condominium. At age 35, she bought her first house, and she now owns three houses in what she describes as premium New York neighborhoods.

Each property represents a cornerstone in her overall plan for retirement, which she expects to do by age 60. Among her properties is a vacation home in the stony Hamptons. The summer rent alone pays the annual mortgage. She has a two-family home in Park Slope, Brooklyn, and an investment property. Her strategy: "I bought in premium neighborhoods where rents were high."

At age 35, Cheryl reached another goal she set for herself. She became a millionaire.

Becoming financially independent—indeed, a millionaire—took "enormous patience, self-sacrifice, and goals I set and stuck to," Cheryl said. "You don't have to be rigid. Always have a dream but exchange and change as you go along, as the picture changes."

Cheryl began steering her future in high school. She decided she needed to go to college and "get educated for a career in a fast-moving field like Wall Street."

Education could not occur at just any school. It had to be credentialed and one that would resonate in her chosen field. She did not want to have a ton of debt on graduation. She got jobs with tuition reimbursement programs and took out no loans. Because of this, she finished her undergraduate degree in six years instead of four, but when she finished, she had no college debt.

It happened just as she planned it. "I did not want to graduate with debt, and my parents could not afford to send me to school. I designed a life that does not incur debt."

When it comes to managing your personal finances, Cheryl says, "You have got to educate yourself. You've got to engage partners who are good at what they do. My physical health is a partnership with my doctor. My financial health is a partnership with my financial advisors. I educate myself so they understand that advising me is a partnership. When they tell me things, I go home and research. I have to live with their advice, so I do my homework."

Cheryl maximizes the percentage she can contribute to her 401(k) and forgets about it. In addition, she determined what she would put into a savings account she cannot get to. "What's left is what I live on." Cheryl also suggests doing automatic deductions. "If you don't see it, you don't feel it."

Cheryl's development of her human capital has helped her find financial peace of mind and economic security. It can do the same for you.

Human capital can be divided into three distinct categories: *intellectual, physical, and spiritual.* Few Americans fully understand human capital and how to use it to enrich their lives. Factoring human capital into financial well-being shows that human capital represents 50 percent of people's ability to reach their financial goals. This means that money has nothing to do with 50 percent of what you need to be financially successful. *Consider this formula:*

Investment capital	25 percent
+ Human capital	50 percent
+ Financial know-how	25 percent
= Financial well-being	100 percent

Much of this book focuses on helping you increase your financial acumen so that you can better manage your investment capital. In this chapter, we discuss the 50 percent of wealth-building resources associated with your human capital. You can enhance your human capital and transform your human capital into wealth by (1) increasing your intellectual capital, (2) protecting your physical capital, and (3) better understanding your spiritual capital.

Intellectual Capital

Intellectual capital is using your mind and consciousness to increase your net worth. This includes placing a value on your education and specialized training. Intellectual capital also includes using your consciousness to attract good fortune and your mental toughness to focus on your long-term goals. Numerous books about the power of positive thinking have added to the general public's understanding and appreciation for the life-enriching powers of the mind. In the following discussion, I explore two wealth-building attributes of the mind that have not been widely discussed:

- The right of consciousness
- Conditioning the mind for financial success

When considering intellectual capital, the first thing that comes to mind is education, especially because earnings rise in proportion to academic advancement. The latest census figures (2000) show the long-term economic return of a college education. Today, the median annual income for an American with a high school diploma earns $21,332; for a college graduate, it is $42,877; and for a person with a master's degree, it is $55,242. A college degree is the best investment Americans can make to increase their intellectual capital.

Reading, with or without a college degree, is also a great way to increase your intellectual capital. Besides being the way many people learn, reading is also a tool people use to become successful. Many successful entrepreneurs who never made it to or through college, are avid readers.

Bill Gates, the founder of Microsoft and one of the richest men in the world, never earned a college degree. But he is not alone. The world is full of successful people who never earned a college degree, but who are very well read, especially in their area of expertise.

Take Don, a successful entrepreneur.

Case Study

He sold his share of a cable operation for a cool $100 million. His entrepreneurial career was filled with many success stories. He had been a successful real estate developer, cable operator, and casino owner. We spoke recently, and he shared with me that this year, his company was on target to earn $300 million. He has achieved all this without a college education.

His secret is that he loves to read financial reports and industrial information. A mutual friend once said, "It is remarkable that despite not having a degree, no one can interpret a financial statement as accurately as he can." Of course, Bill Gates and my friend are the exception and not the rule. Therefore, we must encourage our children to receive a college education.

However, the lesson is clear. If you cannot attend college, you can still increase your intellectual capital by reading. To use a phrase from Dennis Kimbro, "Readers are leaders." According to Dr. Kimbro, "Normally, the leaders in any given fields are there because they have read more and applied their reading more than anyone else in their field" (*Think and Grow Rich: A Black Choice,* Ballantine Books, 1991).

While increasing our financial wealth, it stands to reason that we would want to read more about personal finances, economic issues, and successful people.

A college education, reading, and an openness to learning are obvious ways to increase your intellectual capital. What is not so obvious is the importance of conditioning your consciousness. *Consciousness,* as defined by Webster, is the "state of being aware of something within oneself."

Give special consideration to the phrase "being aware of something within oneself." It suggests the importance of preparing ourselves to experience prosperity and affluence. Could this be true? Do you have to be internally aware of something before you can live it externally? The answer is yes.

The saying "First there is the inner, and then there is the outer," is a valid statement. First we think it, and then we do it. We experience in our mental world before we experience in our physical world. For this reason, many writers suggest that what we experience in our outer world is nothing but a reflection of an earlier thought.

My own observations about consciousness and wealth have helped me understand that everything people own, they own by right of consciousness. Until you are prepared mentally to enjoy a new car, a new home, or a profitable business, you will not have it. Or, if you do, you will not keep it for long.

Conditioning your consciousness for financial success is important because your financial well-being begins and ends in your mind. Your ultimate financial success does not lie in the hands of your employer, your banker, or your government. It depends on the wealth-building thoughts or lack thereof in your mind.

Hence, you need to control the information you admit into your consciousness. Eric Butterworth, a minister and an author, wrote, "Your negative thoughts of fear and worry are depleting your good faster than inflation erodes the value of the dollar. And your positive, optimistic thoughts add to your good more dramatically than compound interest increases your bank savings" (*Spiritual Economics,* Unity Books, 1983).

Conditioning the mind with prosperous thoughts is wise, but in a world where five minutes of the nightly news can provide enough depression to last a lifetime, it is unlikely that you can fill your mind only with thoughts of success and prosperity. Nevertheless, try to reflect on prosperous ideas and thoughts on a regular basis. Read success-focused books, listen to motivational tapes, and associate with people who strive to be prosperous and have a positive view of life.

Computers were created to duplicate the mind by digitizing and retrieving information. But, there is another similarity between a computer and the human consciousness. You cannot expect an outdated computer with outdated software to provide the same information and power as a newer model. Furthermore, computers are only as good as their software and data: If you put junk in, you are going to get junk out. The same holds true for your consciousness.

You must constantly be aware of the junk—wealth-restricting thoughts— that other people try to program into your consciousness. Always deny access to any myths or misconceptions about wealth. Don't program or fill your personal mental computer with limited wealth-building software.

Millionaire in the Making

Gary, a firefighter in Maryland is an excellent role model: He is always updating his mind with new wealth-building information.

Gary is a self-professed "personal finance junkie." He cannot read enough money management books. When a new book is published by one of his favorite financial authors, he not only buys a book for himself but also orders copies for his fellow firefighters. Gary explains, "At the firehouse, I guess I have like a reputation of being the information person. If someone wants to buy a car, he'll come to me and ask me questions on what I think." Gary uses the information he acquires from his studies. He and his wife own their home. They recently refinanced it at a lower interest rate and used the money to pay for renovation. This family has no credit card debt.

Gary friends often tease him about the way he manages his money. But he takes it all in good stride, "I," Gary says, "get teased a lot at work because I'll have money in little envelopes because I divide money into different things, spending or discretionary. And if one envelope's empty, I will not take money from another one. I'll just have to wait until the next pay period." Such discipline helped prepare the couple financially for the newest addition to their family.

"This is our first child," Gary boasts, "I think we're lucky and blessed because we refinanced last year and that allowed us to save money we had earmarked every month. And that allowed us to take care of initial baby expenses."

Gary believes reading more financial books will teach him how to improve his family finances. He thinks that most of the advice in personal finance books is doable. "They're pretty straightforward and direct," Gary says. He is right; many wealth-building books are full of useful advice that is easy to understand. So read as many of them as you can and build a success library. If you view your financial education as an enjoyable lifelong activity, you will constantly be increasing the return on your intellectual capital.

Physical Capital

While expanding our understanding about the relationship between intellectual capital and wealth, we must also explore the relationship between our physical capital and financial success. Three factors could erode your physical capital:

1. The economic impact of preventable illness
2. Failure to view good health as a wealth-building opportunity
3. Underestimating the value of time

Physical capital revolves around a person's ability to earn a living and to make investments. It also revolves around disability, sickness, and death, any one of which could severely jeopardize your family's financial well-being.

Death is the primary factor that denies families the opportunity to substantially increase their net worth. What is most alarming is that many deaths are the result of preventable or treatable illnesses such as cancer, hypertension, heart attack, diabetes, and for a majority of people, obesity.

You can understand the economic impact if you realize that time, no money, is the most important factor in becoming financially successful. Every family needs time to recover from financial mistakes, establish a career, build an investment portfolio, have their children grow up and become independent, accumulate money in a retirement plan, and let financial assets compound and appreciate. Time is especially important if you are only investing a small portion of your earnings every month. Too many people imperil their physical capital by refusing to incorporate healthier changes into their daily lives.

Good health is a wealth-building tool. You can protect your physical capital by safeguarding your health. Think of your health in these terms:

- Longevity nurtures prosperity.
- Good health is the best investment you can make.
- Good health drives your earning capacity.
- Good health gives you a longer time frame to build an estate.
- Good health gives your funds time to compound and appreciate.

It is hard to discuss physical capital and not discuss balance in your life. We all need to have a balance between the time we work and the time we play. We need balance to make sure that we can sleep, exercise, and eat properly. We need balance to make sure that we are truly doing the work that we want to be doing and living the life we want to be living.

My friend Mali, is a successful businessperson who knows the importance of balance in her life. She travels around the world doing business deals, and everywhere she goes, she reminds people to do something nice for themselves every day. "It doesn't have to be a big thing. It could be just taking the time to read a poem, look at a flower, or call a friend. What matters is not the expense but the doing," she says. Mali is reminding people to put some balance into their everyday hectic lives.

Another way to get balance in your life is to find employment or a recreational activity or even a volunteer activity that brings you joy. In our efforts to succeed, sometimes we forget why we are trying to succeed: It is so we will have more life to enjoy. When you are mindful about your physical life, you will find joy when you work and when you play.

You can do this by loving the work (paid or volunteer) that you do. Have you ever wondered why the most successful people are often also the busiest people? One of the reasons is that they love what they do. They often love their work so much that they never get enough of it. So they work constantly.

Warren Buffett, the world's most famous investor and money manager, is one of the richest men in the world. This title alone requires him to lead a busy life, without mentioning the numerous business ventures he oversees. Whenever Warren Buffett speaks, people listen because they know his advice can enrich their lives. He once shared the following advice with a group of eager investors:

> I am really no different from any of you. I may have more money than you. But money doesn't make me different. If there is any difference between you and me, it may simply be that I get up every morning and do what I love to do, every day. If you learn anything from me, this is the best advice I can give you. (Paul B. Farrell, *The Lazy Person's Guide to Investing,* Warner Business Books, 2004)

Do what you love to do—that is the best advice the world's greatest investor shared with this audience. It is also the best advice I can share with you. When you do what you love to do every day, then you will enjoy more of your life every day.

To learn more about bringing more harmony into your life, go to one of the many holistic retreats sponsored by well-known spiritual and medical advisors like Dr. Deepak Chopra (www.chopra.com). There is an open-door policy at the Chopra Center, located in Carlsbad, California. A visit there may transform your life. It is a place to heal, recharge, and reconnect with your spiritual self.

If you want to learn how to achieve more balance in your life closer to home, attend a local seminar featuring Dr. Wayne Dyer (www.waynedyer.com), or Anthony Robbins (www.anthonyrobbinsdc.com). These two well-known body-mind speakers, along with others, can help you learn how to succeed and enjoy more balance in your life.

Spiritual Capital

Spiritual capital is the energy—or lack of it—that emanates from your relationship with a spiritual power and helps you live a prosperous life. All great religions of the world attest, "There is a spirit, or soul, in human beings." You cannot overestimate the value of this spirit, or *spiritual capital,* as I call it. I have met many financially successful people who have attributed their success to a higher power.

Although some people understand and use their spiritual capital to enhance their financial well-being, many people do not. Many people harbor notions about God that undermine their ability to enhance and understand their spiritual capital:

- They may see God as a superbeing living in the sky, ready to punish or reward them depending on their actions.
- They may believe that a life of poverty is a Christ-like life.
- They may view their relationship with God as interpersonal and not intrapersonal. For them, it is a relationship that is outside them and limited, rather than a part of all that they are and all that they do.
- They may view God as a being to depend on, instead of as a being who empowers.
- They may believe that in this world, we must suffer for our rewards in the next world.

Many successful Americans understand and readily use their spiritual capital. Often these individuals have a calming presence. At first, this calmness may appear as confidence, but there is something unique about the way they talk, walk, and act—a demeanor that announces to the world, "I am one with God." Johnny was only a sixth grader but he had already developed a sense of his spiritual capital. One day his classroom teacher saw him frantically drawing a picture. She inquired, "Johnny what are you drawing?" "I am drawing a picture of God," the young student replied. Hearing this the teacher said, "Johnny, you can't draw a picture of God. No one knows what God looks like." The young artist just kept drawing and replied, "they will in a minute." Johnny's response reflects the growth of his spiritual capital. You can measure spiritual capital by:

- The manner in which you face the challenges of daily living.
- The way you demonstrate the principle of love for yourself and others.
- Your understanding that God wants you to succeed.
- How you live and manage your personal and business affairs.
- Your relationships with your family, friends, and coworkers.

According to Reverend Eric Butterworth, the connection between spirit and prosperity is natural. In his book *Spiritual Economics* (Unity Books, 1983), Butterworth writes that the Latin word *prosperus* means "to hope or to go forward hopefully." He concludes, "Considered in the broadest sense, prosperity is 'spiritual well-being.'" Take time to develop your spiritual well-being by embracing the spirit of success within you.

There are many ways to embrace that spirit. You can pray, you can worship in groups, you can be still in any quiet setting. Because the spirit of success is within you wherever you are, you need not worry about going to any special place to find it. Many people have found that meditation helps them connect with their inner selves. Meditation is a way to slow down and allow yourself time to hear your inner voice.

Find a method of being still that best suits you. This exercise may help:

- Choose a relaxing space where you will not be disturbed.
- Breathe in and out slowly.
- Stay still and let your body and mind relax.
- Listen patiently as the still small voice within you speaks to you.

If you are new to meditation, it may take you some time before you feel comfortable with the process. You may even find it necessary to use a meditation audiotape, read a meditation book, or even join a meditation group. All these options are acceptable and can help you discover your spirit of success.

John Bryant is an dynamic entrepreneur, public speaker, and leader in the financial literacy movement. He is the founder of Operation Hope, a national financial education and self-help organization. I always enjoy hearing John give one of his spellbinding talks. Every time I have heard him speak, he has made a point to tell the audience: "Remember, you are not a human being having a spiritual experience. You are a spiritual being having a human experience!" John's maxim explains why it is important for you to embrace the spirit of success. Doing so will help you better understand and appreciate the abundance of your spirituality.

Developing your human capital will prepare your mind, your body, and your spirit to successfully play the wealth-building game. Enhancing your intellectual capital, protecting your physical capital, and embracing your spiritual capital will also help you save your emotional capital and increase your financial capital.

Moneywise Master Class

Religious beliefs have played an enormous role in shaping Americans' understanding of financial success. For this reason, I invited Reverend Floyd Flake, Senior Pastor of the Allen African Methodist Episcopal Church in New York, and Rabbi Marc Israel of the Religious Action Center of Reform Judaism to appear on *Moneywise*. We talked about the connection between religion and money. Here is a portion of that interview:

> **BOSTON:** Reverend Flake, is there a conflict between religion and money?
>
> **FLAKE:** Absolutely not. When you look at a congregation like mine with 13,000 members and raised $9,700,000 last year, the reality is it is not a conflict. We must find better ways to use that resource and in our case, we use a lot of it obviously for social programming. We build homes, we buy up boarded-up vacated property in our community. We build senior citizen centers. We actually built 166 brand-new homes because I think that for most people their primary asset is their home.
>
> **BOSTON:** Rabbi Israel, do you agree?
>
> **ISRAEL:** I agree fully with everything that Reverend Flake said. There is no question that religion and money are not in inherent conflict, at least not within the Jewish faith. We understand that personal wealth can be a very positive thing; the question is: What [do] you do with your money? And religion speaks fundamentally to what people should be doing with their money. The Bible talks about the tithing, that's what we need to do.
>
> **BOSTON:** For a long time, spiritual people have been under the notion that money was the root of all evil.
>
> **FLAKE:** That's a total misinterpretation. It is out of context. The Bible says that the love of money is the root of all evil and I think Rabbi Israel makes it very clear; the issue is not money, the issue is: Where your heart is. How you deal with it. How you make those resources

work. Whether you do that in a just way, a fair way, so that if you are a Christian businessman or a Jewish businessperson, your practices are reflective of your faith. For example, I tell (my church members) give yourself ten percent and then I ask them the question: What do you do with your ten percent? I challenge them to become homeowners because they have to understand the difference between investing in appreciating and depreciating assets.

BOSTON: So there's no need for someone who wants to be spiritual to believe that they must also be poor.

ISRAEL: In fact, within Judaism, we're specifically told that when we are giving, when we are looking at how we allocate our resources, that we're not supposed to impoverish ourselves, because if we do so, then we end up needing to be the recipient of the money that we could be using to help others.

BOSTON: Let's talk about financial education within religious organizations.

ISRAEL: Within the Jewish community, socially responsible investing money has really skyrocketed over the last decade. We encourage congregations and Jewish institutions to invest at least 1.8 percent of their funds in community investment banks.

FLAKE: Well, in my organization, one of the big things we do is investment clubs. We started an investment club because I was doing a men's Bible study with 120 guys and the market hit an all time high that week. I asked the men; What does this mean to you? Do you understand it? You're living in New York (investment capital of the world), and I discovered that only three people in the whole room had investments in stocks and bonds. When I asked them where are your investments? They said, savings accounts, certificates of deposit, and insurance policies. And I said, well go home and read your insurance policy and what you'll discover is that you get three and a quarter to three and a half percent after you die. That was when we decided to start an investment club. Today, we have 12 investment clubs.

BOSTON: Any resistance?

FLAKE: There's not so much resistance as there is trying to understand a new modality, how to deal with a reality of downturn in the stock market. They don't understand that you have to stay in the market and wait for it to come back up.

BOSTON: How do you feel about people praying for money?

FLAKE: (Laughing.) Very good question. I think that this whole notion of ask whatever you will in the Father's name and it will be given—I think it's a sense of optimism to envision the things that you want. I don't have a real problem with it. I think like any other thing you want in life, you pray to God for it.

ISRAEL: (Laughter.) What we're looking at here is the idea that you want people to be praying for their well-being. You want people to be praying to be successful, to be able to have what they need. When money becomes the end game, I think is where you have a problem and people discover that on their own. When you have money as the goal in and of itself, you often find that you're not going to find the happiness that you think that it's going to bring.

BOSTON: What's the one thing that you like for people to take away as it relates to spirituality and financial success?

ISRAEL: That where we put our money reflects very much who we are. And we need to be encouraging people to be looking at how they are investing their money, where they're investing their money, not only in terms of financial gains, but also in terms of how does this promote the values by which I want to lead my life.

FLAKE: Well, I want them to know that there is a connection between heart and treasure and where your heart is, that's where your treasure is. Your heart ought to determine the kind of values, the kind of things that are important in your life, and through that definition, you can have money but you also know how to use it properly, so that not only is it about you, but it's about how you improve the quality of life for other people as well.

These two spiritual leaders make it clear that there is no religious contradiction in being spiritual and being financially successful. Still, just praying for financial success won't make it happen. While you may be heavenly connected, you are still physically grounded. Therefore, you are going to have to build your net worth the old-fashioned way—one human step at a time. In doing so, you will have to make some hard decisions. When those times come, remember the Psalm of Success.

The psalm reminds us that we have a friend who is, according to spiritual advisors, the most powerful force in the Universe. This friend is waiting to help you be all you can be financially. You can call this force God, Nature, Universal Substance, or the Great I Am. The term you use doesn't matter much. What does matter is knowing that when you feel as if you are too tired, too worried, or too anything to continue to pursue your financial dreams, you have a friend that you can call on the lifeline. And this friend will always remind you of the wealth-creating power of the spirit of success.

When faced with a major financial setback or roadblock, just be still for a moment and remember the Psalm of Success written in 1936 by Charles Fillmore (reprinted with permission from the Unity Church):

> The Lord is my banker; I shall not want.
> He makes me lie down with a consciousness of abundance:
> He has given me the key to his safe deposit box.
> He has restored my faith in his riches:
> he leads me down the path of prosperity
> for his name's sake.
> Yes, though I walk through the valley
> of the shadow of debts,
> I will fear no evil:
> for thou art with me;
> his gold and silver comfort me.
> He has prepared a place for me
> in the presence of my creditors.
> He fills my wallet with plenty;
> and my bank account and net worth are growing.
> Surely prosperity and abundance shall
> follow me all the days of my life:
> and I will manage my financial affairs
> in the name of the Lord forever.

Charles Fillmore, the father of the Unity Church movement, created a storm of controversy when he proclaimed, "It is a sin to be poor." Many people took his words literally, but Fillmore was speaking figuratively. He was trying to say that it would be incorrect for a Christian to have a *poor self-image*—a contradiction to believe in the purpose of Jesus Christ and yet believe that this belief compels you to live in poverty.

The thought-provoking works of Fillmore and others (Deepak Chopra, Wayne Dyer, T. D. Jakes) remind us to develop our human capital and experience the spirit of success. Understanding how to develop your human capital will enhance your financial lifestyle and reduce your fear of financial success. Take a few moments to reflect on how to develop your human capital.

MASTER KEYS

Know

**Without the assistance of the Divine Being
I cannot succeed.
With the assistance of the Divine Being I cannot fail.**

—*Abraham Lincoln*

Act

**Start a success library.
Do something nice for yourself every day.
Visit a holistic retreat.
Strive to bring more balance Into your life.
Eat, sleep, and exercise properly.
Love yourself.
Love your work.
Meditate.**

Believe

God Wants Me to Succeed!

3

Planning Your Financial Future

Money is better than poverty, if only for financial reasons.

—*Woody Allen*

Emotional Factor:
Fear of Making Financial Decisions

It will be difficult to win the money game if you are afraid to make financial decisions. Many people find themselves in this dilemma. They want to manage their money better, but they just can't seem to decide what to do. So, instead of deciding what new financial path to follow, they make the worst decision of all. They do nothing at all and force their financial affairs to cruise on autopilot.

I am a big fan of the old Little Rascals short films. We often see these black and white films on the classic movie cable channel. One of my favorite

57

Little Rascal episodes features the character named Buckwheat. In this episode Buckwheat is riding in a motorcycle sidecar. These are the little seats attached to a motorcycle. While driving down the highway Buckwheat's sidecar separates from the motorcycle. When cruising by himself the motorcycle driver shouts, "Buckwheat where are you going?" Buckwheat replies, "Don't know but I am on my way." Buckwheat's travel plans represent how many people manage their financial life. Financially speaking, they don't know where they are going. But they are on their way.

Managing your personal finances can be daunting. There are many investment options, insurance products, and retirement plans to choose from, each with its own risks, opportunities, and tax implications. Still it is far better to take control of your financial resources than to let them take control of you, or worse get out of control.

When Janice thought her finances were getting out control, she didn't stand still. Instead she took responsibility for her financial obligations and control of her financial life.

Millionaire in the Making

Janice is 51 and a vice president and manager for a national mortgage lender. She has an income she describes as "pretty good—more than average" and owns a comfortable townhouse condominium.

Janice embarked on her wealth accumulation strategy approximately 10 to 15 years ago when she moved into senior management and started earning stock options. That got her interested in making other investments as well. But it was a trip to a car mechanic 10 years earlier that had forced Janice to reconsider her economic decisions.

When she got her first decent paying job, Janice made the mistake a lot of people make when they start earning money. She describes her spending spree as a phase that she went through. She bought a brand-new car. She lived paycheck to paycheck, buying what she wanted as long as she had the cash.

It was the car that gave her a rude awakening. Because it needed minor repairs, Janice took her car to the shop. However, when it came time to pick the car up, she didn't have the money. She had to borrow it from her parents. "I said never again. I had mismanaged my money. I made up my mind," says Janice. "I've got to be disciplined here; I need to say no."

Coming from a family of modest means, Janice learned about frugal living from her own upbringing. As an adult, she applied these lessons, developing a habit of careful spending that has helped her find financial independence. She realizes that, even with her high income, she has to be careful in her purchases. As she puts it, true financial security is when you know you have the money to purchase a $1,000 designer handbag, but you buy a $100 bag instead. After all, she says, it's just a handbag. Janice is careful with all her purchases, because she knows that her overall goals are important.

Janice makes it clear that living frugally doesn't mean totally denying herself luxuries. She says you need to find a balance between saving and living well. She plans for the long haul and is disciplined with her spending, "If it's not on sale, I don't buy it," she says. She does, however, make room in her budget for splurges that matter to her. She plans for spa days and takes vacations. "What's important is simplifying my life—looking toward what I need, but still having fun."

Janice is now in a position to meet her financial goals. She is planning to retire early, within the next 10 years or sooner. But her idea of retirement is not like that of her parents, who lead a quiet life. She has a lot of energy and many opportunities. She may open an art gallery when she retires. Financially, she will be in a position to do it because Janice is the captain of her financial ship.

Having a financial plan can help you take control of your financial future.

Professionally prepared financial plans are a great resource for people who are fearful because, when properly executed, the planning process can help fearful decision makers decide what to do. In this chapter, we review how a financial plan can help you take control of your financial future.

To Everything There Is a Season

Like people, every dollar comes into our lives for a reason, a season, or a lifetime. In our relationships with people, we cannot choose our family members or the strangers who enter our lives and become our lifelong friends. In our relationship with money, however, we can choose which of our dollars we will spend in a season and which we will save for a lifetime (referred to as "long-term goals" by financial planners). Long-term goals include saving for college, raising the down payment for a house, or investing for retirement.

Once a dollar is spent, it is gone forever like a season past. So, it is important to hold onto a portion of your earnings in much the same way you would try to hold onto a relationship with a trusted friend.

Understanding how dollars can be divided into seasonal and lifetime resources is important because only funds invested for the long-term can increase your net worth. Hence, when I discuss investing, I refer to investing *lifetime* dollars. These dollars, or funds, would be invested for five years or more.

Most of the dollars we earn remain in our possession for only a short time. This time frame may be hours, days, or weeks, depending on when the monthly bills are due. Hence, most households only have their earnings for a particular season, and few households ever fully benefit from long-term investments.

To substantially increase your family's net worth, you need to identify financial resources that you can invest for a lifetime. By allocating both seasonal and lifetime dollars, you will be acknowledging that there's a time for spending and a time for saving. But more important, because of such allocations, you can enjoy the benefits of having seasonal and lifetime investments.

Case Study

Whenever I consider long-term investing, I remember a story that Joel, a successful entrepreneur, likes to tell. Joel's story begins when he was working part-time at night to complete his college education. He had finished a tour of duty in the armed forces; he was married, with a family; and he was also working full-time at an auto plant during the day.

One day, a security guard noticed Joel's college textbooks and asked him how long it would take him to finish school. Joel told him that he could only take a couple of credits per semester because of his responsibilities. The guard snickered and said, "At this rate, it will take you at least five years to finish your college education." His inflection seemed to indicate that this was a waste of Joel's time.

The unflappable Joel responded, "That's okay, because if I'm lucky, I'll be here anyway." The inference was that Joel would still be living, but living better after having completed his college education. Today, Joel is recognized as one of the most successful and influential entrepreneurs in the United States.

Adopting a long-term investment philosophy can be difficult. One of the biggest challenges is to stay focused on your long-term goals. A financial plan is a tool that can reduce this anxiety and help you stay focused.

The Financial Planning Process

A financial plan is usually a computer-generated document prepared by an insurance or investment professional. These documents evaluate the likelihood of your reaching your financial goals given your age, asset allocation, and tax obligation. Most financial plans concentrate on specific goals such as funding a college education, planning for retirement, or reducing estate taxes.

When your financial advisor returns your plan, it probably will include many tables, charts, and graphics; do not be overwhelmed! What you really want to know is what it will take financially to reach your goals, and what you need to do to get there. The plan will provide the answers. A conscientious planner will take the time to carefully explain and design a plan of action to help you reach your stated goals.

All computer printouts are not financial plans, and all financial advisors are not financial planners. Anyone with a computer and financial software can print out a chart that forecasts financial projections. A sound financial plan is more than just a compilation of numeric charts. It should list your stated goals; give a timetable to reach them; have financial projections related to your stated goals and asset allocation; provide disability, life, and liability insurance evaluations; make investment recommendations related to your goals; and give income tax management strategies. Some of this information will be computer generated, and some of it will be prepared by your financial planner.

The plan is really a tool to help your financial advisor evaluate your financial situation and devise a course of action that will enable you to reach your financial goals. It is much like the way a medical doctor reviews your medical charts to diagnose your medical problem and provide a cure.

Take care when looking for a competent financial planner. In most states, there are no laws for accrediting a financial planner, and many shady characters have used the title to proffer poor financial advice to unsuspecting people. And it isn't only people of moderate means who get taken in. Sadly, it isn't unusual to read about star athletes or entertainers who end up broke because they were so busy making money that they failed to oversee the managers of their financial affairs.

Financial planners are well aware of the bad eggs in their midst and have begun to set standards for legitimate practitioners of the craft, just as doctors and lawyers do.

The Institute of Certified Financial Planners is a leading organization. Practitioners who pass an extensive course in financial planning offered by this organization are allowed to call themselves Certified Financial Planners (CFPs).

At the least, these professionals will have a minimum of competence to address your needs. At best, they can draw on their experience and resources to be an outstanding part of your wealth-building team. The CFP designation, like an MD or JD, is not an absolute guarantee of competence; it is, however, the most widely recognized financial planning credential in use. The Institute is located in Denver, Colorado, and has trained thousands of financial planners, who work independently, at banks, or at brokerage houses.

Since accountants have traditionally been a source of financial advice for people, it isn't surprising that the American Institute of Certified Public Accountants also runs a program for accountants who want to offer financial services. Certified Public Accountants (CPAs) can become Accredited Personal Financial Specialists, who engage in the full range of financial planning services.

The International Association for Financial Planning in Atlanta, Georgia, also will refer you to financial planners in your area. This organization requires less extensive training for its planners because the planners must have advanced training in accounting or insurance.

The National Association of Personal Financial Advisors in Buffalo Grove, Illinois, can refer you to financial planners who work strictly on a fee-only basis. Like accountants, they will charge you only for putting together a financial plan and will not try to sell you stocks, mutual funds, insurance, or other products on which they make a commission.

Finally, the Association for Financial Counseling and Planning Education of Columbus, Ohio, can direct you to a private financial planner who specializes in financial life planning. This relatively new area of financial planning takes a more holistic approach to the financial planning process. Many of these advisors do not limit their financial examination to your financial goals. They will also seek to learn about your financial behavior and emotional drivers.

Financial Life Planning has been defined by its leading advocates in the following way: "Financial Life Planning is an approach to financial planning that places the history, transitions, goals, and principles of the client at the center of the planning process. For the financial advisor or planner, the life of the client becomes the axis around which financial planning develops and evolves. This involves broadening the conversation beyond investment selection and asset management to exploring life issues as they relate to money" (David E. Marcinko, *Financial Planning Handbook for Physicians and Advisors,* Jones and Barlett Publishers, 2005). Table 3.1 shows the various financial advisory organizations along with their contact information.

Several large national companies also offer financial planning services. Two of the largest are Amereprise Financial, formerly known as American Express Financial Advisors, and Merrill Lynch, that's right—Merrill Lynch. Many traditional brokerage services companies like Merrill Lynch offer financial planning services to their customers.

You usually have to be a customer first, but to eliminate that situation, just call and ask the company for its financial planning department. Also, many insurance companies and large banks today have financial planning departments. All too often, these institutions offer more complete financial planning services to their most affluent clients (doctors, lawyers, and entrepreneurs). Still it won't hurt to learn about the financial planning services offered by your insurance company or bank.

Table 3.1
Financial Planning Professional Designations

Certification	Certification Group	Web Site
Chartered Financial Analyst (CFA)	Association for Investment Management and Research	www.aimr.com
Certified Financial Planner (CPF)	Certified Financial Planner Board of Standards, Inc.	www.cfp-board.org www.cfp-ca.org
Chartered Financial Consultant (ChFC)	The American College of Insurance and Financial Advisors	www.amnercol.edu
Master Financial Professional (MFP)	American Academy of Financial Management	www.financialcertified.com
Chartered Asset Manager (CAM)	American Academy of Financial Management	www.fiancialcertified.com
Members hold various certifications	Society of Financial Services Professionals	www.financialpro.org
Certified Financial Planner (CFP)	Financial Planning Association	www.fpanet.org
NAPFA–Registered Financial Advisor	National Association of Personal Financial Advisors	www.napfa.org
Financial Service Specialist (FSS)	National Association of Insurance and Financial Advisors	www.naifa.org
Accredited Financial Counselor (AFC)	Association for Financial Counseling Planning and Education	www.afcpe.org
Accredited Personal Financial Specialist (APFS)	American Institute of Certified Public Accountants	www.aicpa.org

Probably the best way to find a good planner is to ask for referrals from friends and relatives. Then interview at least three prospective candidates. It is important to find a planner you feel comfortable with because you will be working with this person for a long time. Some questions you may want to ask the interviewees are:

- How long have you been in the business?
- Do you specialize in any product or service?
- How are you compensated?
- What services does your company provide?
- Will other members of the company help prepare your plan?
- How many clients do you have?
- What is the average net worth or portfolio of your client base?
- How many of your clients have written financial plans?
- Can I see some of the financial plans you have prepared?
- Ask how many clients have stayed with the planner through the past three years, or five years.

There are no free lunches on Wall Street. You are about to enter a world where you must pay for any services that you receive. Do not expect free advice from anyone, and if it is offered to you, then consider it carefully before taking any action. Most financial planners earn their living from collecting fees for designing financial plans or from commissions they receive for selling insurance and investment products. Either way, you will pay for their services.

There has been a debate in the industry that fee-only planners are more objective than commission compensation planners. My experience has been that it simply depends on the integrity and ability of the planner to always put clients' needs first.

A Great Wealth-Building Tool

Most superior financial tools tend to share the following characteristics: They are easy to understand, lack glamour, and are readily available to the general public. For these same reasons, they tend to be underappreciated. One such tool is a financial plan. Over the years, many people have underutilized this great financial tool.

Many families let their financial plans collect dust on their bookshelves. You could do the same thing, but I suggest that you do not because no other wealth-building tool will be more important than your financial plan. A written plan is the first investment a family should make. It is also the best! Here are some other reasons financial plans are highly desirable:

- They help families clarify and achieve numerous financial goals.
- Families can determine where they are spending their money.
- Financial plans are affordable (ranging from a few hundred to a few thousand dollars).
- They help families develop a sound tax management strategy.
- Financial plans can be tax deductible.
- Families can use their plan as a map to their financial goals.
- Financial plans help organize families' financial resources.
- Spouses can discuss their finances in a nonthreatening manner using a financial plan.
- Financial plans help families understand their real insurance needs.
- They help families understand the financial commitment necessary to meet their financial goals.
- Financial plans are useful in planning major purchases.
- They help determine the most effective way to invest resources.
- They establish the size of a family's estate and net worth.
- They incorporate the financial needs and benefits of small business ventures.

A financial plan is one of the few investments that everyone needs whether you are single, married, young, old, just starting out with a small monthly saving program, or are a high-income earner with a large estate. It does not matter—if you do not have a financial plan, you are not being all you can be, financially speaking.

Designing a Wealth-Building Plan

Financial plans force people to write down their goals. Writing down your financial goals will help you clarify what you want to achieve in life and when you want to achieve it. Having goals also gives meaning to our efforts to save money.

American households use financial goals all the time to plan major purchases. Many people who have never been able to save a dime for anything will find a way to save when they know that they need a few thousand dollars for the down payment for a new car. Suddenly, the goal becomes achievable and saving is not hard to do because they have that goal.

To turn your financial plan into a wealth-building plan, you must add financial security as one of your goals. You will meet this goal when you increase your net worth to $500,000 or to $1,000,000.

Financial Obstacles

Many obstacles can prevent you from reaching your net worth goals. Some of these obstacles include financial risks, taxes, inflation, and living beyond your means. We encounter risks in everything we do. There are financial risks such as premature death, disability, or the need to pay a large settlement as a result of litigation. Proper planning through risk management can reduce the effects of these risks.

Taxes also hinder us. We are taxed on the wages we earn. We are taxed on most interest we receive. Even worse, we are taxed again at death if our taxable estate is too large. We can reduce these risks by proper tax planning and estate planning.

Inflation is also an obstacle to effective financial planning. Inflation constantly affects our cash flow as the prices of goods rise. It has an impact on reaching our goals of college funding and retirement planning. Inflation also impacts the real rate of return on our investments.

Everyday living can affect our planning process. Surveys have indicated that the number one reason people don't plan financially is that they see it as too time-consuming a task. This expression sums it up quite well; "Why do today what I can do tomorrow?" Most people fall into another category where all their intentions are good, they make some plans, but something always happens to detour their efforts. For a young couple, the story goes something like this: "Once we get settled in, we can start to save some money." Then the kids come along, and they say, "Once the kids are grown, we'll really be able to save some money." Then the kids go to college and they say, "Once the kids graduate, we will be on easy street and can save all kinds of money." By then it's time to retire. By getting started on a plan and following it through, we can overcome this obstacle called procrastination.

A good financial plan will help you organize your financial information. Financial plans will help you do the following:

- Gather data and analyze your current situation.
- Determine goals.
- Devise strengths to achieve goals.
- Set a time line for implementation.
- Monitor and review your progress.

Your Financial Success Team

Successfully designing and implementing a wealth-building plan is a team effort that involves you along with your significant other, your financial planner, your legal advisor, your stockbroker, and your CPA. This team will be there to help you successfully execute your plan. But you don't have to wait until you assemble your team to begin the planning process. Here are several steps you can start now.

Your Financial Dream Book

Many people incorrectly believe that money is the factor that separates financially successful people from financially unsuccessful people. In most instances, however, the missing factor is a financial plan. When I was a financial planner, I observed that individuals with a financial plan usually achieved their goals.

Assume that at the present time you do not have a financial plan or a strategy to increase your net worth. Now consider what will happen after you begin the financial planning process. You will have a net worth goal of $500,000 to $1,000,000. You and your financial planner will design financial strategies to help you achieve your net worth goal. And you will have a timetable and a plan to match your goals and income. Maybe now you can understand why, with financial planning, all things are possible.

Furthermore, a financial plan is your family's book of dreams. It is an outline of the financial dreams you have and the steps you are going to take to secure those dreams. In Wilmington, Delaware, where I grew up, it was not unusual to see dream books in people's homes, corner stores, and lottery outlets. These were small paperback books people would use to match their dreams to a winning lottery number. While I saw many people refer to these dream books, I must confess that I never saw anyone hit a winning lottery ticket. In fact, the only dream book I ever saw that helped make a dream materialize was a written financial plan. In the following Profile in Courage, Marsha used a financial plan to help make her retirement dreams come true.

Profile in Courage

Fifteen years ago, Marsha and her husband decided they needed someone to help them invest. They knew they couldn't go it alone. They wanted their money to grow, and they knew that financial planners were "out there," but they didn't know much more about the process. So they got busy.

They called several financial planners and started asking questions. "We asked what their responsibilities were and what ours would be," says Marsha. They also wanted to choose someone with whom they could have a comfortable relationship. "We looked for someone with a good track record, who looked like he successfully invested his own money. We also looked at reputation," Marsha said.

Once they settled on a financial planner, they decided how much to invest each month. Marsha and her husband monitor how they invest, and they also count on their financial planner to keep track as well.

They expect their financial planner to let them know if he thinks that certain investments aren't working out as well as they all had hoped. It is a team effort. In addition to regularly keeping track of investments, Marsha advises also keeping track of your financial planner.

As with any professional relationship, it's time to move on if it stops meeting your needs. This became an issue with Marsha and her husband when they decided that their financial planner wasn't paying as much attention to their investments as they felt he should. So they started making phone calls.

The second time through was easier; they had a better idea of what they were looking for and were able to ask more focused questions. Once they found a new financial planner who suited their needs, they told the first one that they couldn't use him anymore.

Thanks to careful investing over the years, Marsha, 51, just retired this year. She is happy that they prepared so well. "It's fun," Marsha says. "We didn't have to change our lifestyle. We pay attention to where we spend our money, but we still travel and still eat out." By retiring so young, Marsha can pursue a second career. She has parlayed her previous experience as an executive vice president of human resources into a consulting business as an executive coach and motivational speaker. "I am out of the corporate world," Marsha says excitedly, "this work will be on my own timetable."

Marsha realizes that she reached her goals because of proper planning, and she encourages others to do the same.

"I think everyone should have a financial planner," she says. As she explains it, a financial planner helps with long-range goals and plans. Most people are stuck in the present, buying what they think they need or want at the moment, often things that aren't assets. A good financial planner helps you prioritize: "He will help you think about things that you may be doing that aren't helping you reach your goals. He also provides an objective viewpoint and even help you to develop and map out your goals." In addition, Marsha advises that not all your money should be wrapped up with one planner, you should also have other assets, such as a 401(k), an IRA, and a house. "But a financial planner can help you put it all together. Even if he is not responsible for all of your assets, he can still look at the overall picture and give you advice on what to do to maximize your objectives."

With all the good things that a financial planner can offer, Marsha speculates about why so many people are afraid to jump in and start using one. She got over her initial apprehension by simply starting the process. She explains that you can get your feet wet by gathering information. She also suggests that what may hold people back is the fear of getting old. They don't want to think about it, so they avoid it. But with proper planning, your "golden years" can be truly golden.

Unlike Marsha, many people still fail to reach their financial goals despite having a financial plan because they put it away in their desk and forget it. Beth Hirschhorn of MetLife explains why this becomes the fate of too many financial plans:

> Inertia is an incredibly powerful force, especially when it comes to financial planning and financial decisions. We tend to talk about our investment and financial dreams. We talk about them over the water cooler and on the commuter

train but we actually don't take action. There's been a great deal of research done on the gap between information and behavior in this particular category. This research shows that we must urge consumers to break out of their inertia and take action (Beth Hirschhorn, Moneywise PBS Series Interview).

Moneywise Master Class

LeCount Davis is the Executive Principal of LRD Management, a financial planning company in Maryland. He is passionate about financial planning. When he was a guest on *Moneywise* I asked him why he was such a strong advocate of financial planning:

Boston: If a person just wants to start investing in a mutual fund do they still need to have a financial plan?

Davis: My motto is plan before you invest. Everything starts with planning because if you don't know where you're going, you're never going to get there. A financial plan gives you a starting point, a destination, and a road map of how to get to your destination.

Boston: Do people change their plans at different stages in their life?

Davis: Yes. Your investment objectives may be entirely different at 50 than what they were at 30. An investor takes more risk with their investments early in their life. People's financial plans change over time because their objectives change and investment strategies change over time.

Boston: Today, families have to try to reach many financial objectives all at the same time. Can a financial plan help in these situations?

Davis: I think so, because it allows people to see the big financial picture and then decide how taking little steps will help reach their goals. The plan also helps families find a happy medium, because some time there are trade-offs. For example sometimes you are going to plan for college educations and retirement at the same time. So you're going to have to make sure you're doing both of them. Many households turn to a financial plan to help them prepare for several major goals.

Boston: How can the financial planning process help would-be home owners?

DAVIS: Financial planning can help new home buyers understand how much home they can afford. Lenders are not at risk when they lend to unqualified borrowers, the borrowers are. The lenders, when necessary, simply foreclose on the property and sell it to another borrower.

BOSTON: What advice would you give first-time investors?

DAVIS: Plan before you invest. Before you start any saving or investment program have a plan in mind. Then prepare your plan, decide what your destination is going to be, and then seek advice, if you need to, on what financial roads you should take to reach your financial destination.

A financial plan can help you overcome your inertia and reach your destination if you implement its strategies. A financial plan is one of the best tools you can use to face your financial fears. The planning process can help you understand your investment goals and your design for achieving them. Just going through the financial planning process is comforting to many people. It leads you to face your financial fears and take action steps for reaching your financial goals.

Take a moment to reflect on how a financial plan can help you plan your financial future.

MASTER KEYS

Know

Our goals can only be reached through a vehicle of a
plan, in which we must fervently believe, and upon which
we must vigorously act. There is no other route to success.

—*Pablo Picasso*

Act

Think of your plan as your dream book.
Have a team of financial advisors.
Design a financial life plan.
Don't invest without a plan.
Planning will help you take control of your future.
Planning will help you overcome fears.
Take action on your plan recommendations.

Believe

I am the master of my economic destiny!

PART TWO

Mastering Financial Success

Most of us aren't interested in getting rich—we just don't want to get poor.

—*Andy Rooney*

Success in money management is not a windfall that comes to some and not to others because of fate, chance, or luck. Success in money management can be predicated (yes, predicated!), if you have a plan and if you follow that plan.

—*Venita VanCaspel*

All our dreams can come true—if we have the courage to pursue them.

—*Walt Disney*

To be ambitious for wealth, and yet always expecting to be poor, to be always doubting your ability to get what you long for, is like trying to reach east by traveling west . . . no matter how hard you work for success, if your thoughts are saturated with the fear of failure, it will kill your efforts, neutralize your endeavors, and make success impossible.

—*Charles Baudwin*

"Bumstead, your problem is that you worry too much about money. Money can't buy you happiness, you know." "Has it brought you happiness, Boss?" "Yeah, but that's just me."

—*Blondie Comic Strip, Washington Post, 2002*

A man is a success if he gets up in the morning and gets to bed at night and in between does what he wants to do.

—*Bob Dylan*

4

MANAGING YOUR CREDIT

When Americans use credit they are often spending money they don't have.
On things they don't need to impress people they don't even like.

—*Tavis Smiley*

EMOTIONAL FACTOR:
Fear of Taking Responsibility

This chapter shows you how to effectively manage your credit. Many Americans never really come to grips with how much they spend each month because they know that they are spending more than they earn. Most of this extra spending occurs from the use of credit. Knowing how to effectively manage your credit will help you reduce your financial fears and reach your financial goals.

Unwise credit usage has limited many people's ability to effectively play the financial game of life. Ill-advised credit management decisions often result in people being denied access to economic opportunities, not because of the color of their skin or the content of their character, but only because of a score on their credit report. The credit score has emerged as the most important determinant in the credit-granting process. Frederick Douglass, an African American statesman, was right when he said, that we "may not get everything that we pay for; but we must pay for everything that we get." We must all pay for everything that we purchase. However, individuals with low credit scores must pay more for their financed purchases.

Credit

It is hard to live in a credit-oriented society without credit. Without credit, you can't buy a car, get a good job, secure a college education, buy a house, get a business loan, rent a car, shop on the Internet, or even reserve a hotel room. We should also keep in mind that it is one thing to have access to credit and not need it versus needing credit and not having reasonable access to it.

Having access to credit is becoming so important that the president of a leading credit counseling firm recently said on a national television show, "Every American teenager who graduates from high school should have a voter's registration card in one hand and a copy of their credit report in the other hand." We should keep this in mind. The more interest and fees you pay to borrow money, the less money you have to invest. To win the millionaire game, you will want to keep your credit report spotless and your credit score high. This will keep your borrowing costs low and enable you to have more income. Here's an example. A borrower with a low credit score can secure a $125,000 home with a 30-year mortgage at a 12 percent interest rate. This borrower's monthly mortgage is $1,285 (principal and interest). In 30 years, that borrower would pay $462,875. Another borrower with a high credit score can secure a $125,000, 30-year mortgage with a 7 percent interest rate. This borrower's monthly mortgage is $831 per month (principal and interests). In 30 years, this borrower would pay $299,386. The monthly mortgage payment difference of $454 a month adds up to $163,488 over a 30-year period. Additionally, this $454 a month could have been used to save for a college education, build up a pension plan, or invest in other investments. This is $163,488 we could have used elsewhere to increase our net worth. Today, all of us have a choice to make. We can choose to have our money work hard for our creditors by continually borrowing money. Or we can choose to have our money work harder for us by paying ourselves the money we would pay to our creditors. You must decide what game plan you will use to win this part of the money game. The game plan you use will ultimately affect the way you live the rest of your life. Know, too, that the most affluent individuals use their credit wisely. Additionally, when they use their credit, they try to use it to make purchases that will increase their net worth. If you are going to win the financial game of life, you may have to follow the same rules when using your credit:

Rule 1: Keep your future credit report spotless.

Rule 2: Use your credit wisely.

Rule 3: Use your credit to increase your net worth.

Understanding basic credit management concepts will help you make informed credit decisions. For me, it's all about ways and means. If you don't know the way, then you won't have the means. Evan Hendricks, author of *Credit Scores & Credit Reports: How the System Really Works, What You Can Do* (Privacy Times, 2004), writes, "In the American consumer economy, the worse your credit score, the more you pay for mortgages, loans, credit cards, and insurance. Conversely, the better your credit score, the more favorable terms you will get on interest rates and insurance premiums."

It's part of a relatively new reality referred to as "risk-based pricing." Hendricks explains, "In the old days, creditors would either approve or disapprove you for credit. Now they don't want to reject you. Instead, they want to grant you credit at the rate that compensates for the 'risk' reflected in your credit history" (*Credit Scores & Credit Reports,* Privacy Times, 2004, p. 2). The good news is that everyone can improve their credit histories and credit scores. It may take a little time and discipline, but it can be done.

Millionaire in the Making

Often when I speak before a live audience, I like to share the courageous story about a young single mother named Faye. She was a widow with two children and desperately needed a new car. But when she tried to purchase a new car, no auto dealer would finance her purchase.

Concerned, she secured a copy of her credit reports so that she could find out what was on them. She contacted all three credit-reporting agencies and found out that her reports contained pages and pages of negative information. Faye could have let this information discourage her, but she chose to use this information as a call to action.

She made a decision to manage her credit more effectively and to improve her credit score. She made a list of everyone she owed money to, and started paying off her debts in a timely manner. She also made a list of every dime that she spent. She wanted to know where all her money was going. She made her teenage children do the same thing. She didn't want them to make the same money mistakes she had made.

It took some time and a lot of discipline, but Faye's work paid off. In time, she purchased the used car she wanted. But since she had improved her credit score, she could also secure a mortgage. So she purchased a small home for herself and her two children.

Faye's credit management situation may not represent yours, but it may remind you of someone you care about. If you must counsel someone facing a major credit crisis, describe Faye's profile in financial courage. Then tell them about the time a young businesswoman applied for a small business loan. After reviewing the woman's credit report, the banker said, "Miss, your credit history looks pretty bad." "Yes, I know," she replied, "But my future credit report is spotless." Your future credit report is spotless, too. Credit scores are used to predict how a consumer would repay a loan. Your credit past and your credit future need not be the same. But keep in mind that no single score means an individual borrower will default on a loan. Only the borrower knows his motivation, willingness, and ability to repay a loan. Where credit is concerned, the borrower could be like a famous home run hitter who pointed his bat to the fence where he planned to hit his next home run. Where your credit is concerned, you can call the shots.

Everyone has an opportunity to call their future credit shots. You can decide to hit a home run or a foul ball. Your hit will be determined by how you hit or miss your future credit repayment obligations. The due payments you hit or miss will greatly impact your ability to win the financial game of life. Here are financial moves that will help you manage your credit. Practice these swings regularly, and you will consistently hit game-winning home runs with your credit management skills.

Know Your Score

A financial game guide must review the topic of keeping the score. What is different about the financial game is that the score you must track—your credit score—may help you secure assets to win the game. But never forget that net worth values are the major indicators of success; and therefore, are more important than credit scores.

Still, we may not be able to secure our primary wealth-building assets such as homes, college educations, and small businesses without debt financing. Furthermore, the less we pay in finance interest and charges, the more money we will have to purchase other assets. Therefore, it is important to know your credit score.

How Credit Scores Are Determined

A credit score is a number that reflects your creditworthiness at any given time. For most credit reporting agencies, the higher the score, the better the risk. People with higher scores often can obtain mortgages, credit cards, loans, and insurance at more favorable rates. Conversely, the lower the score, the less favorable terms will be in any offer. The score is often based on the data in your credit report. Each credit reporting agency has its own credit score. So your score may vary, depending on which credit-reporting agency you or your lender uses. The general scoring range is 300 to 850. The Fair Isaac Corporation, a leading developer of credit-scoring models, divides the scoring range into five risk categories:

1. 780 to 850—Low Risk
2. 740 to 780—Medium-Low Risk
3. 690 to 740—Medium Risk
4. 620 to 690—Medium-High Risk
5. 620 and Below—High Risk or "Subprime"

Credit score models are well-guarded trade secrets of credit-reporting agencies. Nonetheless, Fair Isaac has released enough information to give a general idea of the factors that determine your credit score. Your payment history accounts for 35 percent of your credit score, your outstanding indebtedness accounts for 30 percent, and the length of your credit history (the longer the better) accounts for 15 percent. New credit lines (10 percent) and types of credit, such as mortgages, credit cards, and finance loans (10 percent), complete the score.

All creditors use different credit-scoring systems. It is possible to be granted credit from one creditor and denied credit from another, based on identical information. Creditors are not required to reveal your scores, and they may use whatever scoring system they choose, as long as they don't discriminate. Institutions use your credit report to formulate your credit score and predict your ability to repay a loan in a timely manner. If your total exceeds their passing score, then you will more than likely be extended credit; if it falls short, you will be denied credit.

Credit Reports

Because credit scores are based on information in your credit report, it is up to you to maintain a satisfactory report as well as monitor it for errors. You should review your credit report two times a year for errors, deletions, or additions that cast an unfavorable view on your credit history. It is estimated that approximately 100 million Americans have incorrect data in their credit reports.

Many times, there are errors in reporting figures. For example, your credit card balance may be $200, but your credit report might show $2,000 by mistake. Also, if you have been divorced, you will want to check your credit record to make sure your personal credit history is reflecting only your own past and current obligations.

In some cases, your report may contain negative records that don't even belong to you! Credit agencies handle a tremendous volume, and errors can occur. Some negative information can stay on your credit report for 7 to 10 years. So even if you haven't had any problems with late or missed payments, it is recommended that you review your credit report on a regular basis.

Free Credit Reports

Under the Fair and Accurate Credit Transactions Act (FACTA), consumers can request a free annual credit report via phone, mail, or Internet. Here are the toll-free phone numbers, mailing addresses, and web sites for ordering your report from the three major credit reporting agencies:

1. Equifax: www.equifax.com
   To order your report, call: (800) 685-1111 or write: P.O. Box 740241, Atlanta, GA 30374-0241.
2. Experian: www.experian.com
   To order your report, call: (888) 397-3742 or write: P.O. Box 2002, Allen, TX 75013.
3. Trans Union: www.transunion.com
   To order your report, call (800) 888-4213 or write: P.O. Box 1000, Chester, PA 19022.

Each credit reporting agency will charge you a small fee for a credit report after you have received your annual free report. Credit agencies will also charge you an additional fee to send you a copy of your credit score. If you want to know more about credit scores you can visit Fair Isaac at www.myfico.com.

Reading a Credit Report

When you receive your credit report, it should include instructions for interpreting it. This information may look overwhelming at first, but it is well worth your while to understand your own credit report. When reviewing it, make sure the information you see is accurate and up to date.

Credit Cards

Studies show that Americans on average have 12 credit cards. Creditor counselors believe that this is too many, and contributes to people becoming heavy credit card users. These same credit experts believe that most people only need two or three credit cards. Credit cards can either be your friend or your enemy. If you pay your credit cards on time and in full each month, then you will have 30 days of the finance company's money. If you allow your credit cards to reach high, unpaid balances, however, they can cost you thousands of dollars and easily destroy your credit history. Here are a few tips to help you use credit cards wisely:

- Avoid making new credit card purchases.
- Limit yourself to two or three cards.
- Pay off balances in full each month.
- Leave cards at home when you shop.
- Plan ahead when you will use the cards.
- Always pay more than the minimum payment.
- Plan to pay off large purchases in three monthly installments.
- Use a debit card whenever possible.
- Do not think of credit cards as emergency funds.
- Don't use a credit card to purchase anything unless it is within your monthly spending budget.

Credit card companies make more money, the longer you take to pay off the debt. So pay off your credit card debt as quickly as possible. The best way to avoid and reduce credit card charges is to pay bills on time and, when possible, in full.

Stay Current

To assure favorable reporting of your account, you should always make your payments on time. Mail your payment a couple of days before the due date, or if possible, personally deliver the payment to the creditor by the due date to assure your payment is received on time. Most credit companies charge a late payment fee for payments not received by the due date.

If you must make a late payment, try to make at least a partial payment by the due date. Always make a phone call to explain your tardiness. Finally, when you receive a statement, always make sure your payment has been credited to your account.

If you have a serious credit problem, go to a credit counselor. She can help you design a budget and plan to reduce your debts. Many can even work out payment arrangements with your creditors.

Living Debt-Free

People often ask me how much consumer debt they should have. The answer is, as little as possible! Many lenders rarely give credit to consumers who have more than 20 percent of their income obligated to debt payments (excluding mortgage payments). Becoming debt free is a worthwhile goal. Some households actually maintain a debt-free lifestyle. With discipline, this goal can be achieved although it is hard to see why people should not finance large expenses like a home or car with borrowed funds. Still, if you want to go this route, you should know the process, which is very simple. Your first step is to stop incurring new debts. Next, make a list of all of your creditors based on the size of your debt. After you make your list of creditors, determine your current minimum monthly payment on all these debts. Your next step is to start using the same dollar amount monthly to pay off your consumer debts.

Rapid Debt-Repayment Plan

Rule 1: Incur no more new debt.

Rule 2: Pay the same amount every month on your debts and credit cards even if the minimum required amount goes down.

Rule 3: List your debts according to their size, putting the shortest payoff time at the top of the list and the longest payoff at the bottom.

Rule 4: As one debt is paid, take the same payment and add it to the regular payment of the next debt on the list. Continue to do this until all your debts on the list are paid off.

Rule 5: After all your debts are paid off, use the same amount that you were paying on the debts and save in it in a savings account, mutual fund, or personal pension plan.

This plan can help you reduce your debts and increase your net worth at the same time. If you use the rapid debt-reduction plan, you will quickly pay off your debts. Once you have reduced your debts, use the savings to invest in your mutual funds and other investments. For example, assume your monthly credit card obligations totaled $640 a month. The rapid debt-reduction program would allow you to pay them off in 5 years. If you continued to just pay the minimum payment every month it would take 32 years to pay off your debts. The rapid debt-repayment plan would give you 27 years to let the same $640 payment work for you. If you saved $640 a month for 25 years and earned 10 percent a year, you would accumulate $762,870. That is how you can use the income you have right now to reduce your debt and at the same time increase your net worth.

You Need Not Repeat Your Past

Financial institutions often make people feel that their true self-worth is tied to the current status of their credit report. It is important for you to understand that a credit report, credit score, or credit history cannot validate your humanity. Credit reports are great at showing what happened in the past, but they cannot predict what will happen in the future.

Although a credit score may give some insights into the likelihood that a borrower will repay a loan, these reports cannot reflect potential changes in people's credit habits over time. Everything changes when you realize that you have the power to control your debts and overcome your fear of doing so. That is exactly what happened to Frances.

Profile in Courage

When you meet Frances, her pleasing personality and loving demeanor let you know that she is one with God. At 56, Frances is currently putting the finishing touches on a new custom-built million-dollar home that sits on 2.15 acres outside Memphis. How did this one-time welfare mother get to this point? No, she didn't win the lottery. Through the various events in her life, she followed her personal motto: "I can do that." Looking at her poise and style, you could never guess the financial difficulties she's endured in a life-long pursuit of financial independence.

Frances admits that she got a relatively late start; she didn't start focusing on wealth accumulation until five or six years ago. Her story demonstrates that it is never too late to achieve success once you set your mind to it—and have enough determination and grit.

She got off of welfare 20 years ago (at age 36) when she became a hair stylist. Eventually, she purchased her own salon. However, while her business was successful, she didn't develop a wealth accumulation strategy. When she was in her 30s, she bought a house. That experience got her to think about changing careers. She realized, as she says, "I can do that."

So she went to school to get her real estate license. The transition was a little slow, and without a savings base to see her through, she ended up unable to make the payments on her house and had to file for bankruptcy protec-

tion. Ultimately, her gamble paid off and she became successful selling real estate in her hometown of Memphis. She attributes her success (she is a top seller for her real estate firm and a member of the multimillion-dollar sellers club) to the business network she had built during her beauty salon days— and, more important, to her drive and ambition. "I have that competitive edge of wanting to be the best," she says.

Once the bankruptcy cleared (a bankruptcy stays on your credit report for 10 years), Frances thought she was home free. She started getting credit card offers and even went out and bought a new car. However, she quickly found out about the dangers of credit and interest rates when she realized that those new credit offers had come with a hefty price.

"I learned. I read books. I went to seminars on how to clean up your credit," she says. She got a copy of her credit report and worked to improve it. She got rid of all her credit cards, except one that she keeps for car rentals, hotels, and such.

Frances also realized that she could do more than simply sell homes. With her improved credit, she and her husband (she has been married now for seven years) started buying investment properties. They now own 12 income properties. All these properties are profitable—the rents they bring in more than offset the mortgage payments.

Part of her success comes from the teamwork with her husband. While she has the real estate savvy, he is handy with a hammer and nail. Together, they started a second business to manage their real estate holdings. They purchase fixer-uppers and, with three employees, quickly repair and clean them up, increasing their value. According to Frances, if the roof and foundation are solid and the house is made of brick, they see potential in it for refurbishment. Because the labor is done in-house, they incur lower expenses than they would have if they had to hire contractors.

Her real estate goals are simple. They own 12 properties already and plan to buy two or three houses per year until they have acquired 50 properties.

With their real estate business well in hand, Frances recently turned her attention to her savings. She has started IRAs and SEP-IRAs and has a 401(k) through her real estate firm, but she realizes that at this late stage, these vehicles will not accumulate enough savings to see her through retirement. But she isn't worried. She is having too much fun working right now to stop, and she feels that what she is building through her real estate portfolio not only will see her and her husband through their old age, but will provide a legacy for their children and grandchildren.

Frances is very goal oriented. She writes down her long-term goals and keeps them where she can see them. And every year, she sets the bar just a little higher for herself. At the end of each day, she sits down and writes out her plans for the next day, what she needs to do, who she needs to call.

"I feel I am at the top of my game, but I still have a long way to go," says this one-time welfare mother who is about to move into her new home in an exclusive gated community. Like many spirit-led people, Frances would not let her financial setbacks keep her from pursuing her desire to become successful. Many nights, Frances turned to a higher source for help and guidance. Her meditations helped her develop financial peace of mind and a will to stay the course. Frances turned to a higher source for guidance because she knew that there was a natural connection between the spirit of success and prosperity.

When Frances decided to take responsibility for her financial life and manage her credit more effectively, her financial life changed for the better. To do the same, you may want to visit PRBC.com. The acronym *PRBC* stands for "Payment Reporting Builds Credit." It is the first and only national credit bureau that enables consumers to show on-time payments of monthly bills that are not reported to the "big three" national credit bureaus: Equifax, Experian, and TransUnion. These bills may include apartment rent, private mortgages, mobile home payments, utilities, phone, day care, self-storage, parking, rent-to own, and insurance premiums.

PRBC allows a consumer to get the credit they deserve for the past three years of bills they have paid on time, as well as the bills they pay each month on time in the future. It represents a profound new choice and set of do it yourself (DYI) tools that consumers never had available before. PRBC is the only credit bureau that does not require consumers to go into debt to show they are willing and able to pay bills on time.

History is the past, lived. But for those who have courage, it need not be revisited again. You do not have to revisit your past credit history. You can move forward and go from credit card to debit card.

You can go from being a day late and a dollar short with credit obligations, to paying your debts a day early and always having a dollar to save. You can go from fear of not having enough to pay your bills, to becoming fearless in your ability to manage your debts. You can go from being an overwhelmed, uninformed consumer to becoming an informed consumer who reduces indebtedness and increases savings.

Moneywise Master Class

Mr. Luther Gatlin is the president of Budget and Credit Counseling Services Incorporated in New York City. He has been counseling people on credit matters for over 20 years. When he was a guest on the *Moneywise* program, he shared the information he has used to help his clients manage their credit effectively:

> **BOSTON:** Luther why is knowing how to manage credit so important?
>
> **GATLIN:** Good credit is important because it determines what kind of financial opportunities will be available to you. It's not just fundamental, it's like breathing. I mean, you can't live in America without good credit. Good credit affects you in every walk of your life. Most people think credit affects you only as you go to get a credit card or buy a house. But you have to realize, to get a job, the first thing an employer does is pull up your credit report. If your credit history is bad, you're not going to get that job. If your credit is bad, you're not going to get that apartment. If your credit is bad, you're not going to get that education. So credit is a basic fundamental. People ask what's the most important thing to have: your driver's license, your Social Security card, your birth certificate? Huh-uh, your credit report.
>
> **BOSTON:** There's a lot of misconceptions about a term called *bad credit;* then we have *impaired credit;* and you have everything in between. And most people become stigmatized. Who is having problems in our culture today related to credit?
>
> **GATLIN:** Everybody, people we see earn $10,000 a year or half a million dollars a year and everything in between. So it's everybody. There's

no stigma to a certain race of people or a certain class of people. It's everybody. I've seen people that make hundreds of thousands of dollars a year who are in trouble. Many people at one time or another have had a credit challenge. How you overcome the credit challenge, is by facing the truth about your finances and getting help from a credit counseling service.

BOSTON: How can credit counseling services help?

GATLIN: A reputable credit counseling service can help you put together a credit repayment plan and help you stick to that plan to overcome your credit challenges. But most people are quite frankly afraid of their credit. They're afraid to know what their credit profile looks like.

BOSTON: Can you tell a good credit counseling service from a bad one?

GATLIN: Yes, credit repair companies that charge up front to "remove" derogatory data from a consumer's Equifax, Experian, or TransUnion file in the absence of a legitimate dispute (i.e., the derogatory information is actually legitimate, but the credit repair company sends a barrage of dispute letters in the hope that the statutory time limit of 30 days will expire before the creditor or credit bureau responds).

BOSTON: Does America today have a crisis when it comes to credit?

GATLIN: No. I say no because I've been doing this for over 20 years; it's been the same. I find the lifestyle of people is what determines whether you're in trouble or not. And I've heard people say that—for instance, people are in trouble when times are bad. Baloney. People are in trouble more when times are good than when things are bad.

BOSTON: How much credit are you suggesting people carry?

GATLIN: Well, I don't think you can put a dollar number on it. It depends on your income. There's a lot of factors involved. The question is really how many credit cards should a person have? The average American carries 12 credit cards, and you don't need them. You really need two or three credit cards, and that's all.

BOSTON: What about the 20 percent rule many credit counselors suggest?

GATLIN: Right, when you get to 20 percent you're in trouble. No more than 20 percent of your income should represent that level of debt, not including your mortgage.

BOSTON: What should people look for in terms of interest rates when it comes to credit cards?

GATLIN: The first thing you should do is, if you already—you have a credit card right now that you're happy with, call that credit card company and say to them, "Look, my interest is too high, reduce it or I'm going someplace else." You'll be shocked how fast they will change it, if you're a good customer.

BOSTON: What should consumers know about their credit report and credit scores?

GATLIN: Remember, every bit of negative information that goes on your credit report, including missing one payment, stays on your credit report for seven years. And most consumers think that because the statute of limitations of seven years has passed and you didn't pay it, it's going to go away. No, it's not. A creditor can put it on your credit report three times. So for 28 years a negative piece of information can stay on your credit report and impact your credit score.

BOSTON: Luther, do you find many of your clients are, in a sense, inheriting their credit management skills from their parents?

GATLIN: No doubt about it. If the family was a family of savers, they are, too. On the other side, if the family wasn't, they're not. The greatest lesson we can teach our children is how to wisely use their money.

BOSTON: Is the credit scoring system we have in place fair?

GATLIN: Who said it's supposed to be fair? Fair is not in this game at all. If you think the credit system is fair, forget about it. It's not fair. It's not designed to be fair. It's designed to make money. You have to realize this. Look, the quality of life for most Americans would not be what it is if it wasn't for credit.

BOSTON: My friend, what would be the one thing you want people to take away from this discussion?

GATLIN: Understand how important credit is, because it is very, very important, and to use it and use it wisely. And learn how to save. Save if it's only $5. Saving is the most infectious thing in the world. No budget works without paying yourself first. You have to realize, when people are in financial trouble, they can't eat. They can't sleep. They can't have sex. They can't do anything because of this mountain of debt. So you have to learn how to deal with it.

You can sense Luther's commitment to helping people effectively manage their debts. His final thought during this interview has always stayed with me. "When people are in financial trouble, they can't eat. They can't sleep. They can't have sex. They can't do anything because of this mountain of debt." That is what can happen to you when you are in financial pain because of being in denial about your financial life. What was Luther's advice? "Learn how to deal with it."

Well, that is exactly the focus of this chapter. Now take a moment to consider how managing your credit can relieve your credit-related anxieties.

MASTER KEYS

Know

Out of debt, out of danger.

—Proverb

Act

Sign up for PRBC.
Keep your future credit report spotless.
Know your credit score.
Use credit to Increase your net worth.
Use a rapid debt reduction program.
Seek professional help if you need it.
Only keep two credit cards.

Believe

I am the captain of my financial ship!

Becoming a Homeowner

People who can least afford to pay rent, pay rent.
People who can most afford to pay rent, build up equity.

—*Arthur Blach*

Emotional Factor:
Fear of Change

For many people, there is something about owning a home that makes them feel secure. Maybe it has to do with the idea that they have control over what can and cannot happen in their space. Maybe it is the sense that they are investing in real property that they own, instead of in some landlord's property. Or maybe it is the sense of planting roots in a community. I don't know what it is about home ownership that can stir a person's soul, but I know that most people long for the day when they will enjoy both the emotional and economic benefits of owning their own home.

Some Americans, however, dread relocating to another house or apartment, and just the thought of inquiring about home ownership sends them into a panic. This is what some financial behaviorists refer to as a fear of relocating. I refer to it as a fear of change. Not only will this fear keep you from moving to different living quarters even if they are better, it will also keep you from becoming a homeowner even if you know that you can afford it and that it would be a good long-term investment. Over the years, this fear forces renters to invest millions of dollars in other people's investment property instead of investing it in their own.

This chapter explains why and how home ownership can increase your wealth. This information can also diminish your fear of changing your status from a renter to a homeowner. Many Americans have made this change; Donna was one of them.

Profile in Courage

Donna, 55, works for a nationwide financial services company. She is also a real estate mogul who has accumulated wealth through smart real estate investing.

Donna, who has owned property in as many as five states at the same time, started small. She inherited a property from her parents in the late 1970s and immediately thought, "What am I going to do with this thing?" That "thing" started her on the road to real estate investing.

"There's wealth in real estate," she says, "but you have to know the right time and the right market." Donna moved to the East Coast from Los Angeles two years ago and is now studying the opportunities and potential markets in her new location. She eschews the hot markets in the current real estate boom in favor of smaller markets.

Instead of looking at what is trendy, she looks at places with an eye to the future. She focuses on areas where the market is depressed so that she can buy into properties at a lower price. That way she feels that she can be a part of the development in the area and increase her wealth at the same time.

"Rome wasn't built in a day," she says, "and your fortune won't be either. You have to take your time." Patience is key to letting your investment grow and mature. Donna keeps her properties for an average of 3 to 5 years, but no more than 10—the length of time that one can keep depreciation on the tax books. She knows that it is important to keep in mind how her investment activity may affect her tax return.

When her daughter went away to college, Donna sent her off with a solid understanding of credit and wealth accumulation. Through a program known at the time as "kiddie condos," Donna purchased a townhouse for her daughter in Virginia. Instead of paying dorm fees, Donna made mortgage payments (which she could deduct from her taxes). Putting her daughter's name on the title gave her daughter instant good credit. And, when her daughter finished college, she was able to sell the condo and have seed money for graduate school.

These life lessons in credit, saving, and building an economic base served her daughter well. Now 32, married with two children, and a social worker, her daughter has maintained her excellent credit score. She and her husband own their own home and several rental properties.

Donna has also laid the foundation for her own retirement at 65, by setting aside money in 401(k)s and annuities. Her future plans do not include real estate. While she will own her own home, Donna does not want to use real estate income to supplement her retirement income. "That's a job," she says, and when she retires, she doesn't want to have to work.

Donna remembers her own beginnings and advises others to start small. You don't have to invest in a lot of high-priced properties right away to get a start in real estate, and you don't have to have a lot of seed capital. You can buy just one property, even if it's the smallest on the block, and you will be in the real estate market.

The Economic Joy of Home Ownership

Owning a home can increase your net worth. Historically, the value of real estate appreciates over time. If you select a home carefully and maintain that home, over time you should be able to sell it for more than you paid for it. This, coupled with the tax deductibility of mortgage interest payments, makes home ownership an effective way to increase your family's net worth.

In your financial plan to increase your net worth into the range of $500,000 to $1,000,000, you will have to include the equity you build in your home over time. But if building equity in your own home is not enough of a reason for you to stop renting, consider this exercise. Add up all the money you pay for rent—for example, $1,000 per month, which equals $12,000 a year. In 10 years, you will have invested $120,000 in your landlord's real estate. Now multiply this by three. This will give you $360,000. This is how much money you will have invested in your landlord's real estate over a 30-year period. When you consider the amount of money you invested in your rental unit, you will realize that you in fact purchased a residence; it just wasn't yours.

The primary issue is whether to invest in your own property or invest in someone else's. Most financial planners will tell you that it is best to invest in your own. After 7 years, it often does not make good economic sense to rent. Now let's suppose that 10 years later, you want to send your child to college, retire, or buy a business. Can you ask your landlord for a loan or to return some of the money you gave him in rent payments? No. If you own your home, however, you could use a portion of the equity to finance your endeavor. If you decide to move and sell your home, you could probably make additional money from your accumulated equity. Once you leave a rental unit, you have no profit to take with you. You can take your personal belongings, but you must leave the money you invested in the rental property behind.

People who successfully play the wealth-building game always try to get a good return on their money. When renting, you are not giving your housing dollars a chance to work for you. Those dollars don't appreciate, nor do they receive any tax benefits. The bottom line is that with home ownership, your money works for you, but in renting, it does not. Hence, the smart money move is to use your housing dollars toward home ownership.

Because home ownership plays a major role in increasing a family's net worth and maximizing the return on the money invested, no one should let financial barriers deter them from buying a home. When house hunting, keep in mind that there are many great neighborhoods to invest in. Second, remember that many banks, mortgage companies, and savings and loans are willing to give you a mortgage.

In addition, governmental and private organizations will help you secure your first home. Many cities have housing departments—they sell lots and vacant or abandoned housing units. The Department of Housing and Urban Development (HUD) has local and regional housing counseling centers that will help you determine how much house your family can afford. The national credit counseling centers can also guide you in clearing up any credit problems, review your budget, and help you qualify for a mortgage. Contact information for these agencies appears in the Resource Guide of this book.

Home ownership unlocks the door to financial success. A well-chosen home will provide you with a comfortable place to live and raise your family. It is a key part of any strategy to increase your net worth.

You can deduct the interest on your mortgage payment, as well as local property taxes. If you have chosen your neighborhood well, your property will appreciate, and as you pay down your mortgage, you can see your equity accumulate.

Yes, buying a house can be expensive. Most homeowners factor in their mortgage payment, insurance, and taxes when determining a budget. They know that there are one-time expenses involved in buying a house, such as moving, closing costs, and mortgage points.

Yet the ongoing expenses of running a house—the painting, upkeep, and repairs—are often a surprise. In some sections of the country, purchasers of new homes must buy their own major appliances. If their budget doesn't cover those costs, what could be a wonderful move into a new dream house might turn into a disaster when the proud owners discover that there is no refrigerator or clothes washer.

The most daunting obstacle facing many families who are attempting to buy a home is accumulating money for the down payment. The good news here is that you may not have to accumulate nearly as much as you thought. Thanks to Fannie Mae and Freddie Mac, two organizations that provide liquidity and affordability to the housing market, you can purchase a new home with only a 3 percent down payment. In many cities across the country, you may qualify for a no or low down payment mortgage. These programs are designed to help low- and moderate-income families purchase their first home. They are often supported by special grants from the U.S. Department of Housing and Urban Development (www.hud.gov). Some of these programs will also offer you a low interest mortgage if you complete a certain number of hours in new home ownership counseling. Such programs may represent the best home ownership buying opportunities in your city. So if you qualify for one of these programs, by all means take advantage of it.

However small the amount may be, you will still need to have some cash to buy a home. So here are five ways to secure a down payment and closing costs:

1. *Open a special down payment savings account.* To help establish this account, you can use your income tax refund.
2. *Earmark your annual bonus.* Earmark any annual bonus you receive for your new house account.
3. *Cash in your cash value life insurance policies.* If you have a life insurance policy with cash value accumulated in it, you could earmark those funds for your new house.
4. *Take money from your tax-sheltered accounts.* If you have a 401(k) plan, Tax Shelter Annuity (TSA), Individual Retirement Account (IRA), or a profit sharing or stock ownership plan at your place of employment, consider using these funds for a down payment. Self-directed retirement plans such 401(k) plans and TSAs have special loan privileges for purchasing a house. But you must be careful when using retirement accounts: All of them have tax penalties for early withdrawals. However, don't let this keep you from using these funds for your down payment.

    Meet with your plan administrator and financial advisor to get the facts so that you will not trigger a tax penalty when you access these funds. This is a viable way to secure money for your new home down payment.
5. *Secure gifts from your friends and family.* In the past, banks were leery of prospective borrowers who showed up with large amounts of money for a down payment when they had relatively low-paying jobs. It was a problem for immigrants where family members pooled their money to buy homes. But, the rules have loosened considerably and lenders are willing to accommodate customers who can show that they are putting up some of their own money or that the money is really a gift. Mortgage lenders want to make sure that the borrower is not overextended with another loan.

How to Choose a Home

Property acquired for use as your personal residence obviously has to meet a variety of standards. It should be a good value, be well constructed and designed, and have appreciation potential. For a personal residence, inspection of the premises by a qualified professional is necessary; you should know exactly what you are getting. The most significant part of buying a house as a personal residence is the fit to your lifestyle. Does the property have enough bedrooms, bathrooms, and storage space? How about proximity to shopping or work? How are the schools? When asked about investing money, actor Will Rogers once said, "I'm buying real estate; they aren't making any more of it." Remember that you and your family are unique, as is every piece of property in the world. Try to make sure you complement each other.

You may also buy a house by renting it first. This type of purchase is called *rent with option to purchase.* There are several variations of this type of purchase, but basically, you decide to rent a house with a contract that will allow you to purchase it for a set price at a future date, usually 24 months. During that time, you make rent payments, and a small portion is designated for your down payment. Another benefit of this type of rent-to-own program is that you can use any appreciation in value to pay for your closing costs when you finally purchase the house. There are several ways to structure a rent-to-own home purchase. For this reason, you should have a real estate lawyer review any documents before you sign them. You want to make sure that if, for some reason, you decide not to purchase the property, you will have a right to sell it to someone else.

Most likely you will borrow the money for your house either from a commercial bank, a mortgage banker, or a thrift or credit union. You'll usually get your mortgage either through the broker who helps you find your house or through the lending institution. Many lenders now prequalify loans, meaning that you can shop for a house knowing beforehand exactly how much you can spend. I recommend that you do this. Some lenders will give you a preapproval letter that also locks in an interest rate for your mortgage, tells you how much they will lend you, and gives you a date by which you must complete the transaction.

Shopping for a new home with a preapproval letter is fast becoming the norm, because this tells borrowers and realtors how much house you can afford. Yet many people still shop for their home the old-fashioned way. They choose a home, then they try to secure a mortgage. In either case, you have to go through the home-buying process. You must agree on terms with the seller of the property and secure a mortgage.

Do Your Homework

Do your homework on value early in the process. Is the price comparable to other homes in the community? Is the asking price above or below the market? Many times, recent house sales are listed in the local newspaper. Home sales are also recorded in county courthouses.

Sellers usually price their property higher than what they really desire. Why? Because they have selling costs, brokers' commissions, and so on. Also, usually sellers would like to get as much equity (investment) out of the property as possible. This means selling the property for as much as they can get. Still, depending on the market, you can usually find a house that will meet your household's needs and represent a good value.

Homes Are Investments

Consider again how you can use your home to increase your net worth. Assume that the home you purchase only appreciates 3 percent in value every year (the average rate of inflation). At this rate, your home value will increase by 15 percent in 5 years and 30 percent in 10 years. I know that in recent years, some hot real estate markets in the United States have appreciated in value by 30 percent in one year. But from the perspective of a long-term investor, any annual appreciation greater than 3 percent would be considered icing on your real estate cake.

Suppose you purchased a $200,000 home with a 5 percent down payment of $10,000. You will have a $190,000 mortgage. In 5 years, with a 3 percent appreciation, your home would be valued at $230,000. In 10 years, your house would be valued at $260,000.

During this 5-to-10-year period, you have reduced the amount of your mortgage. What would the results be in 10 years if you decided to sell this house?

Sale Price	$260,000
Mortgage	$175,000
Equity	$85,000

This will give you enough money to put 20 percent down on a $400,000 home. Now you will repeat the cycle of the 3 percent appreciation, only on a $400,000 home. In 10 years, this house's fair market value will be $520,000.

This is a simplistic scenario, but you see my point.

Due to the leverage and the compounding impact of inflation, home ownership can unlock the door to financial success. Understanding this wealth-building concept is important because ideally, what you want to do is to take the equity out of your house when you retire.

At that time, you may be over the age limit of 55 years, at which time you will not have to pay taxes on your real estate profits.

So you can use your equity to buy a nice retirement condo for you and your spouse, and invest the remaining funds in your retirement account. By the way, with just a 3 percent annual appreciation rate, you will have more than $320,000 in equity that you can use toward securing your retirement condo and retirement savings.

To reach this goal, you must treat your home like a real estate investment and not just shelter. You may have to be willing to sell your home every 7 to 10 years if it does not appreciate at a 3 percent annual rate. This gives you enough time to pay down your mortgage and experience some appreciation in the value of your home. This strategy will also allow you to double the amount you pay for your second home, should you decide to purchase one. Keep in mind that you will have a larger down payment, so you will be able to keep your monthly mortgage rate within your budget.

While your first down payment might have come from savings, tax returns, or friends, the second down payment will come from your existing equity. Due to your second home's greater cost, you will probably see more appreciation in its value than you saw in your first home.

Moneywise Master Class

Marcia Griffin is the president of HomeFree-USA, a nonprofit housing counseling service in Washington, DC. She was kind enough to appear on the *Moneywise* program and share her tips for first-time home buyers. Here is a portion of my interview with Marcia Griffin:

> **BOSTON:** Where can new home buyers get good, sound advice? Any suggestions?
>
> **GRIFFIN:** They can go to an experienced real estate agent, who really can be your best advocate. Otherwise you're self-represented, which is a dangerous place to be, at least I think it is, and a real estate agent can guide you through the process. She can help you with a lender; it's a lot more than just driving by a house and opening the front door and saying, do you want to buy it?

BOSTON: Anything else people should think about before they get started in the home buying process?

GRIFFIN: Make sure that the credit report is in good shape and then really start doing a little bit of research. I would certainly encourage home buyers to ask their friends, what did you do wrong? What would you have done differently? The other point is to try to save as much money as possible. Hold onto as much money as you can and really continue to save because you will need money to buy a home even if you do get a loan that's a zero down.

BOSTON: Now, Marcia what can you do if there are some errors on your credit report?

GRIFFIN: I would not be discouraged from purchasing a home. You may end up paying a slightly higher interest rate, but rates are so low right now it shouldn't stop you from buying a home just because you've got something on your credit report.

BOSTON: A lot of people like to buy apartment buildings—just maybe a duplex, but still it's an apartment building.

GRIFFIN: The good thing with a two to four unit apartment building is that you can generally use the same mortgage product that you can in buying a single family home. Once it gets beyond that, then it becomes commercial property and it's a much bigger investment.

BOSTON: Any rules of thumb about refinancing that you think people should know?

GRIFFIN: Two points below your current [interest rate]. If you are at 7 percent and you can get one at 5, go ahead and do it. That rule of thumb doesn't hold so much anymore. I think the main thing I would suggest to people when you're refinancing is get a loan with no points. For tax purposes, points on a refinanced loan must be amortized over the life of the loan and you cannot take them off in one lump sum on your taxes as you can when you purchase.

Owning a home is a great way to maximize the return on the dollars that your family spends on housing. It is also a great way to help increase your family's net worth. Anyway you look at it, owning a home, a condominium, or a co-op is a major step in facing your home ownership fears and building your home ownership wealth.

MASTER KEYS

Know

Success is to be measured not so much by the position that one has reached in life as by the obstacles which he has overcome.

—Booker T. Washington

Act

Make a list of reasons owning a home would be better than renting.
Know how much house you can afford.
Visit with a housing counseling service.
Save money for your down payment.

Believe

Home ownership can help increase my new worth.

BECOMING A CONFIDENT INVESTOR

Pennies don't fall from heaven; they are earned on earth.

—*Margaret Thatcher*

EMOTIONAL FACTOR:
Fear of Financial Loss

You can reduce your fear of losing money in the stock market by learning how to invest in equity investments, specifically equity mutual funds and investment clubs. Financial experts agree that know-how is the best way to counteract the fear of investing, which often involves the fear of losing money or making a money-losing decision. People tend to fear what they don't know. If you don't know how to invest in stock investments, you are likely to be fearful of the process.

To reduce your fears, this chapter focuses on improving your investment acumen. Investment know-how alone is not a guarantee against a financial loss. From time to time, even the world's best investors experience less than stellar performances and make poor investment decisions. However, their knowledge limits their losses and helps them reach their financial objectives. Understanding how stock investments can fund your dreams can do the same for you. This financial knowledge will show you how to reduce your anxieties (related to financial loss) and substantially increase your net worth.

While this chapter reviews several stock investment options, our primary focus is on mutual fund investing and stock investment clubs. These two opportunities are well suited for fearful investors. Both allow you to increase your earnings without exposing your initial principal to enormous risks. Both are easy to use and understand. Both allow you to pool your resources with others. But more important, both allow you to learn more about investing in stocks before you start purchasing individual shares. Small investors have used mutual funds and investment clubs to build small fortunes.

Some people may wonder why a book written to help working-class households increase their net worth would have a chapter on investing in the stock market. These skeptics would probably say that hard-working families earning less than $75,000 annually are not interested in investing in the stock market. To these naysayers, I have but one reply, "Nonsense!" Every year, millions of Americans increase their wealth substantially because they own stocks and securities.

Furthermore, I don't remember reading in the U.S. Constitution that only affluent Americans should own appreciating assets.

Investing in the stock market with its wealth-building opportunities is not the exclusive domain of the rich. The reality is that the stock market is for any investors who, according to Benjamin Graham, "expect a reasonable return on their investments without being exposed to much risk." Graham, considered by many to be the father of modern-day stock analyses, once stated, "An investor is one who, after careful analysis, expects an investment operation to promise safety of principal and adequate return" (*The Intelligent Investor,* HarperCollins, 2005).

When referring to investors, Graham gives no preferential treatment to anyone based on income, age, gender, or race—nor should he. If there is one thing we know about financial investments such as stocks and bonds, it is that they are void of prejudice. These investments perform their stated tasks regardless of their owner's income, education, or gender.

Why You Should Invest in Stocks

There are four chief reasons many Americans have not routinely invested in the stock market:

1. They do not think that they have enough money to invest in the stock market.
2. They are not aware of their investment options.
3. They are too busy trying to survive to think about investing for the long term.
4. They are afraid that they will lose their savings in the stock market.

Although all these reasons are valid, none of them justify losing the bene-fits of one of the world's greatest wealth-building tools—shares of publicly traded growing companies. In many ways, owning stock offers the same economic rewards as being self-employed. The basic difference is that in-stead of running the business, you invest in it and share the company's for-tunes—good or bad.

We live in an age of new and great economic opportunity. Most of these opportunities are connected to the social changes around us. Consider the Internet . . . the cell phone . . . the computer. Each represents new technolo-gies with new investment opportunities. You must always be looking for such opportunities; therefore, you must always have money on your mind—at least part of the time. A quick review of the historical performance of the stock market illustrates why such thinking can be financially rewarding.

Figure 6.1 illustrates that over a long time period, stocks are one of the best places to invest your money. The average return is 12 percent com-pounded annually. This return is better than most investment options, and it helps preserve the purchasing power of your earnings.

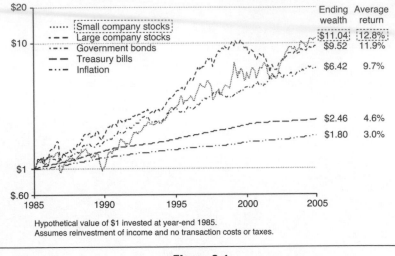

Hypothetical value of $1 invested at year-end 1985.
Assumes reinvestment of income and no transaction costs or taxes.

Figure 6.1
Stocks, Bonds, Bills, and Inflation, Year-End 1985–2005

This is for illustrative purposes only and not indicative of any investment. An investment cannot be made directly in an index. Past performance is no guarantee of future results (March 1, 2006). Copyright © 2006 Ibbotson Associates, Inc. Reprinted with permission.

Figure 6.2 illustrates that the best way to reduce your risk in the stock market is to invest for 10 years or more. The longer you invest in the market, the greater are your chances to earn a profit of 12 percent compounded annually. The risk of stock market loss over time is shown in Figure 6.3.

Still, many people try to avoid investment risk by investing their money in "sure things" like bank certificates of deposit (CDs), fixed retirement accounts, and life insurance cash values. Unbeknownst to these investors, the financial institutions often invest the money from the CD in the stock market. Most banks, pension plans, and insurance companies have a large portion of their assets invested in the stock market. They do so to earn a 12 percent return. These shrewd financial organizations then credit the "sure thing" investor's account with, let's say, 2 percent interest, keeping the additional interest (10 percent) as profit for their stockholders.

It is easy to see why many financial planners believe you should always try to maximize the return on your investment. By doing so, you have a greater chance of not only making more money, but more important, pro-

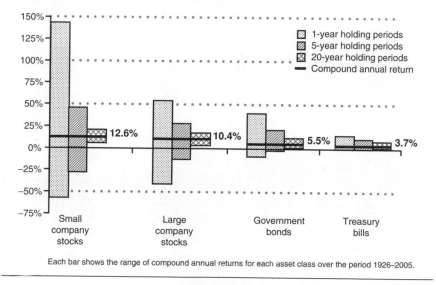

Each bar shows the range of compound annual returns for each asset class over the period 1926–2005.

Figure 6.2
Reduction of Risk over Time, 1926–2005

This is for illustrative purposes only and not indicative of any investment. An investment cannot be made directly in an index. Past performance is no guarantee of future results (March 1, 2006). Copyright © 2006 Ibbotson Associates, Inc. Reprinted with permission.

tecting your future earning power. Historically, the stock market has been one of the best investments to increase personal wealth and protect your income from inflation (see Figure 6.1).

Theodore J. Miller drives this point home in his book, *Invest Your Way to Wealth* (Kiplinger Books, 1994). Miller writes, "If it's wealth you want, look to the stock market. No other investment available to intelligent amateurs with average resources, average willingness to take risks and limited time to spend on active management delivers as well as stocks over the long run. . . . Stocks aren't the only things that belong in your investment portfolio, but they are the most important."

Types of Investments

Before you invest, you must first understand your investment goals. No one investment can accomplish all your goals. Your financial portfolio should include several investments, each targeted to meet a particular goal. If you

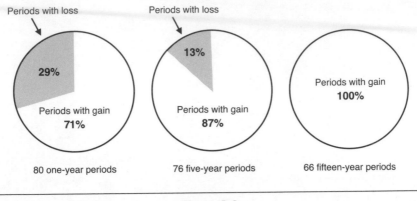

Figure 6.3
Risk of Stock Market Loss over Time, 1926–2005

This is for illustrative purposes only and not indicative of any investment. An investment cannot be made directly in an index. Past performance is no guarantee of future results (March 1, 2006). Copyright © 2006 Ibbotson Associates, Inc. Reprinted with permission.

wanted to acquire an emergency fund, you would probably want something safe, liquid, and easily accessible. A savings account at the credit union might meet this need. If you had a long-term goal, you might choose a stock mutual fund. These funds tend to do well in the long run. And if you were striving for retirement income, you might choose a bond mutual fund that would generate income to supplement your retirement income.

Stock Ownership

Stocks are equity investments. When you own stock in a corporation, you are one of the owners of that corporation. This ownership provides investors with the possibility of dividends plus appreciation, or growth, of the share price. As the value of the corporation increases or decreases, the value of the stock reflects the change. Americans who have never invested in the stock market sometimes wrongfully equate investing to gambling. You do not have equity ownership when you purchase a lottery ticket; put coins in a slot machine; or make a bet at a racetrack, in a card game, or on your favorite sport team. In other words, you do not own the lottery machine, the slot machine, the casino, the racetrack, or the sport team.

Only a few gamblers are lucky enough to win, thereby getting a return on their bet. The odds are normally against the gambler ever winning any sizable amount of capital.

Stock investors, however, not only have their capital investment, they also have an asset that may increase in value. Additionally, a team of corporate officers is always working for them. Yes, I have heard about Enron and the other major corporations whose corporate leadership forgot that they were working for their investors. But these companies represent only a few bad apples in an orchard filled with thousands of ripe opportunities. Therefore, prudently investing in stocks and gambling have nothing in common. There are speculators in the stock market, but most of these people are professionals. The majority of investors are long-term investors, and usually they are also the most profitable ones. The point is that investing in the stock market is not akin to gambling. Gambling is a game of chance, but stock market investing is a claim to corporate ownership.

Kinds of Stock

People often ask me to explain the stock market. As its name implies, it is a market where investors can purchase shares of corporate stock. Only corporations can issue stocks. Partnerships, sole proprietorships, and limited partnerships cannot issue corporate stocks. Stocks are traded on three major stock markets: the New York Stock Exchange (NYSE), the American Stock Exchange (AMEX), and the National Association of Security Dealers Automated Quotation System (NASDAQ). Stocks sold on the exchanges are often referred to as *listed stocks,* whereas stocks traded on the NASDAQ are usually referred to as *over the counter* (OTC) stocks.

Four Direct Stock Investments

Many stock brokers do not want to deal with small investors, and they will not tell you about investments that may be better suited for small investors because these options offer the broker only a small commission, if any.

The direct stock investments most commonly used by small investors are company stock plans, personal retirement plans, dividend reinvestment plans (DRIPs), and investment clubs. All these investments allow small investors to buy shares of major companies without investing a large sum of capital.

Company Stock Plans

Company stock plans let employees buy stocks on a weekly or quarterly basis. They can purchase one share at a time or have a percentage of their salary applied to purchase certain stocks on a regular basis. Often, employees can purchase their company's stock without a charge.

There was a time when all major companies encouraged their employees to purchase their company stock, and companies often gave stocks as an annual bonus to their employees.

Personal Retirement Plans

Personal pension plans are primarily Individual Retirement Accounts (IRAs) and 401(k) retirement accounts. Most brokerage firms will allow small investors to purchase shares of common stock with a relatively small investment. Brokers prefer to trade stocks in whole lots, that is, 100 shares. An IRA investment of only $500 to $2,000 may not be enough to purchase 100 shares, but the brokerage firm will still allow you to purchase odd lots—that is, less than 100 shares of stock—for your IRA or other personal pension plan.

Dividend Reinvestment Plans

DRIPs are dividend reinvestment plans offered by almost 900 companies. They allow current shareholders to purchase stock directly from the company, bypassing brokers and their commissions. Most of the dividend reinvestment programs allow investors to reinvest their dividend at no charge. There are several ways to join a DRIP. You can contact the company directly, or you can contact the three organizations listed here:

1. The National Associations of Investors Corporation (NAIC)
   Telephone: (877) 275-6242
   Web site: better-investing.org
2. Moneypaper
   Telephone: (800) 388-9993
   Web site: moneypaper.com
3. First Share
   Telephone: (800) 683-0743
   Web site: firstshare.com

All three of these organizations will charge you a small fee ($5 to $20 per share) to purchase one share of stock on your behalf. After you have purchased your first share, you can begin to make optional cash investments and build a portfolio of blue chip companies.

Investment Clubs

Investment clubs represent another way many small investors are investing in the stock market today. Americans participate in investment clubs to enhance their knowledge about investing and increase their individual net worth.

Profile in Courage

Ken Janke is the president of the National Association of Investors in Royal Oak, Michigan. Ken, we like to say, not only talks the talk, he walks the walk. He learned how to build his multimillion-dollar stock portfolio by participating in investment clubs. The knowledge he gained also prepared him to serve on corporate boards and oversee other people's investments.

Ken says that the one question about investing that people ask him most frequently is "When is the right time to get into the market?" Over the years, he has always given the same answer: "Twenty years ago, but it's never too late." Ken started investing in the 1960s by creating an investment club with a group of friends. "I just started calling old friends from high school." Ken says. His friends called other friends, and they pulled together about 15 people. Even though they were all fresh out of college and busy starting families and careers, each member put in $10 to $20 per month. "We all learned together," he says.

The experience set him on a lifelong path toward investing. Over the years, he has observed investment groups and counseled others in starting groups. Ken says the best way to organize a group of 12 to 15 people is to call a few friends, colleagues, or other associates and have them also call others who might be interested. That way, there is not one dominant person in the group—everyone is on the same footing. Initially, a typical investment club may have only one person with investment experience outside the club. But as soon as five years later, the balance shifts, and almost all the members also engage in their own investment activity outside the group.

An investment group offers more than just a social experience or an opportunity to pool resources, although these are significant benefits. They also offer a peer community of learning. "Too many people are intimidated," Ken says, and if they are investing solo, they may be afraid to ask questions. But in an investment club, he says, "You are learning together; if you don't know, you look it up." And with several people sharing in the research, everyone benefits. An investment club creates an environment where there is freedom to explore and learn together.

To those who are afraid of investing, Ken says that the best way to learn is by doing, so just jump in. You have to have some money at risk, even if it's only $10 to $20 a month. "But you also have to have the right attitude," says Ken. "You have to have a long-term view." You can't worry about what the market is doing day by day or even week by week; keep yourself centered and focused on the future. "You aren't going to get rich quick, that doesn't happen," Ken says, "People get rich slowly."

Funding Your Dreams

The National Association of Investors Corporation (NAIC) provides guidance to investment clubs. Over the years, the NAIC has developed a highly beneficial investment approach based on four principles that consistently aim at long-term capital appreciation: (1) invest regularly, (2) reinvest your earnings, (3) invest in growth companies, and (4) diversify to reduce risk.

Invest Regularly

It is virtually impossible to find anyone who has built a fortune over a lifetime by forecasting short-term movements in the stock market. In contrast, millions have profited from purchasing sound stocks regularly because the stock market has always increased in value over the long term. When you invest equal sums of money at regular intervals, such as monthly, semiannually, or annually, you are using the technique of *dollar cost averaging*. This means that you will buy more stock shares when prices of the stocks are lower, and fewer shares when the prices are higher.

Dollar cost averaging is the primary tool small investors have to make money in the stock market. This system levels off the peaks and valleys of the share prices and works best if practiced over the full business cycle for at least five years. Regular investing lets investors increase their holdings, even when the market is high. It also frees them from trying to compete

Table 6.1

Advantages of Dollar Cost Averaging

Investment ($)	Example 1: Fluctuating Market		Example 2: Rising Market	
	Price/Share ($)	No. of Shares	Price/Share ($)	No. of Shares
50	4.0	12.50	4.0	12.50
50	5.0	10.00	2.5	20.00
50	6.0	8.33	1.5	33.33
50	7.0	7.14	1.0	50.00
50	8.0	6.25	2.0	25.00
50	9.0	5.56	4.0	12.50
Total Shares		49.78		153.33
Final Price		× $9.00		× $4.00
Value		$448.02		$613.32

with professional investors at market timing. The examples in Table 6.1 show the advantages of dollar cost averaging in fluctuating markets.

Even when investing larger lump sums, you should establish a systematic (monthly) investment program and not worry about whether the market is up or down. This reduces your cost per share without having to know the right time to buy. Although dollar cost averaging has definite advantages, it cannot assure a profit or protect against loss in declining markets. Investors should consider their ability to continue to invest in periods of low-price levels, and for the long term.

Reinvest Your Earnings

Companies pay out their annual profit in the form of dividend payments, which are similar to interest payments. Many investment clubs try to realize a 4 percent to 6 percent dividend yield from the company they invest in and reinvest the earnings to produce a compound rate of return. In essence, they buy more shares of a company with that company's profits. These reinvested dividends, along with appreciation in the value of the company stock, help investment clubs enjoy stock market success.

Invest in Growth Companies

A company must attain growth over a period of years to warrant that designation. Many investment clubs only consider companies that have a five-year history. Management is the most determining factor of growth. Many seasoned investors believe that growth is most reliable when produced by management, as opposed to industry growth, or universal product growth.

Investment clubs try to identify companies that have shown growth in the past and are positioned to continue growing in the future. To recognize growth-oriented companies, investment club members review s company's annual reports to find out if it has experienced consistent growth in sales, consistent growth in earnings, and a superior return on stockholders' equity.

Diversify to Reduce Risk

Investment clubs are advised to invest one-fourth of their funds in major companies, one-fourth in small companies, and the remaining half of their portfolio in midsize companies between the two extremes. By following these guidelines, investment clubs can experience a rate of 8 percent to 10 percent in price appreciation.

Coupled with dividends, this allocation enables investment clubs to attain a 14 percent overall return. The goal of the investment club is to average 12 percent to 14 percent annually.

The Value of Becoming an Informed Investor

The great thing about the NAIC's principles for stock market success is that, if followed, they help small investors become informed investors who research their companies before they invest their money. Investment club members understand that no stock will be purchased without a standard analysis and report on the company in question. Although not expected to become professional analysts, members are proficient in applying some important tests to assist the club in becoming successful in buying and selling stocks. Their research also helps them stay the course should the overall stock market decline or the economy experience a recession. Informed investors don't let market or economic conditions overshadow their investment decisions about a company. Instead, when market and economic factors change, they look at the reasons for their stock purchase, and make a decision to hold or fold.

If, on the one hand, the company is still doing well or as expected, then informed investors keep their investment. If, on the other hand, the company is not performing well, they may decide to trade their holding for a new one. Investing time to become informed can help you become a better stock investor. I was reminded of this concept whe viewed Peter Lynch, the former fund manager of the Fidelity Magellan Fund. He is considered one of the greatest stock pickers and money managers of our time. During this interview, Peter shared one of the major reasons for his success, "You must know what you're investing in. Never invest in any company that you can't explain with a crayon," he said. In other words, if you don't fully understand the business your company is in, then maybe you are investing in the wrong company. Peter Lynch points out that being an informed investor is your best tool for achieving success with direct stock investments. For those who want to learn more about Peter's successful selection of stocks, I highly recommend both his books, *Beating the Street* and *One Up on Wall Street* (Simon & Schuster, 1989).

Few people are aware that individuals can become members of the NAIC and take advantage of the investment advisory services. To join, call (877) 275-6242. For additional information about direct stock market investing, you may also want to contact the American Association of Individual Investors (AAII). This organization provides information to small investors who want to make their own stock market investment. They can be reached by calling (800) 428-2244. For a nominal annual membership fee, you will receive their monthly newsletter, the *AAII Journal,* several annual stock market investment guides, and membership in a local AAII chapter.

Mutual Funds

Mutual funds are growing in popularity as average investors look for ways to buy into the stock market. With professional investment management and a diverse array of holdings, mutual funds help small and large investors alike increase their investment portfolios. Saving for retirement and college tuition are the top two reasons for investing in mutual funds. However, many people use mutual funds to put aside money for a down payment on a house, save toward a family vacation, or just increase their net worth.

Case Study

Mutual funds are a good choice for novice investors like Marshall, a single young professional embarking on a successful career track. Marshall believes

Mutual Funds are right for him citing, "I am young and I can take a little risk with my money but I'm worried about investing in individual stocks on my own. For me, I think to start mutual funds are the safer way to go. Once I learn more about investing in the market, I will eventually invest in individual stocks. But I believe that right now, since I'm early in the game, that a mutual fund would be a better choice for me."

Diversification and active management of the portfolio are the key reasons to invest in mutual funds. If you have $50 a month that you're investing, you can't go out and buy individual shares of corporate stocks. But you can buy into a mutual fund and automatically own shares of many corporate stocks. So it's a good way to diversify your investments.

Many people do not want to be bothered with all the work associated with researching, managing, and trading individual stocks. These investors may prefer a mutual fund. They offer many of the same benefits of direct stock investment, but without a lot of the work. You still have to select a mutual fund that matches your long-term goals and has a good track record, but the process is less time-consuming and complex than selecting individual stocks. In fact, next to performance, convenience is probably the major reason that mutual funds are the most used method of indirect investment in the stock market today. (Other ways that Americans invest indirectly in the stock market are through pension funds, variable life insurance policies, and variable annuities.) Mutual funds are an ideal investment for small investors for several reasons.

When investors use mutual funds, they pool their money with other inventors to buy a large portfolio of stocks or bonds. In general, mutual funds offer an investor the following benefits: diversification, professional management, liquidity, and convenience. All mutual funds offer their investors diversification. Most mutual funds take the pooled resources and purchase several hundred stocks from various companies. By doing this, the fund tries to protect the value of the portfolio. To diversify simply means to own many investments instead of a few.

Mutual funds offer professional management and administration at nominal fees. Managing investments can be complicated. Mutual funds can provide the management without the high costs of buying separate equity or debt investments. You give up a small percentage of your investment to have mutual funds provide this service. Another benefit of investing in mutual funds is liquidity. Many investors like knowing that they have access to their funds. Mutual funds are readily redeemable either by the fund (open-ended funds) or on the open market (closed-ended funds). The mutual funds are redeemable for the net asset value on the day requested.

The biggest benefit of mutual funds is convenience. Many have low investment requirements and will allow investors to begin with only a small monthly payment. Additionally, mutual funds offer systematic investment plans with bank authorization, investment prospectuses, annual reports, transfer services, and accurate record keeping. Some will even let you invest without paying a front-end sales charge. Like stocks, there are a variety of mutual funds to help investors match their investment goal with the correct type of fund. The Investment Company Institute classifies mutual funds in 22 broad categories, according to their basic investment objectives.

Primarily, mutual funds are similar to stock and bond investments, so the categories include cash, growth, growth and income, balanced, index, international, and tax-free income bond funds.

While there are more than 22 mutual fund types, you may only need a few to reach your financial goal. To increase your net worth over time, you may choose only to invest in a balanced fund, an index fund, and an international fund. Balanced funds generally have a three-part investment objective: (1) to conserve the investors' initial principal, (2) to pay current income, and (3) to promote long-term growth of both the principal and income. Balanced funds also have a portfolio mix of bonds, preferred stocks, and common stocks. The balanced fund will offer you growth opportunities without exposing your assets to much market fluctuation. This is a conservative move, but as you become more experienced in investing in the stock market, you may decide to become a more aggressive investor.

The second type of fund to consider is an index fund. These funds invest in stocks that match the stock market index they are trying to track—the S&P 500, the S&P 100, and the Dow Jones Industrials are the most popular. The fund managers' basic goal is to match the return of the index they are tracking. Index funds are considered a conservative way to hitch a ride on the market.

The third type of mutual fund you may want to consider is an international stock fund. International funds invest in equity securities of companies located outside the United States. Two-thirds of their portfolios must be so invested at all times to be categorized here. For added diversification and opportunity, many financial advisors agree that some portion of your portfolio needs to be invested outside the United States.

These three types of mutual funds can help you reach most of your goals, but you still need to know how to select the right mutual funds. Table 6.2 provides a selection of funds for research and possibly investment. Use the phone numbers provided in the table to order prospectuses and other research information, and review them carefully before investing.

Selecting a Mutual Fund

Before investing in a mutual fund, you must first identify the goal you want that fund to help you achieve. When selecting a mutual fund, as with selecting a stock, you always want to match the fund objective with your investment goal.

If your primary goal is to increase your net worth in 10 years, you want mutual funds with the potential for capital appreciation.

Because you may be investing only a few dollars on a regular basis (dollar cost averaging), you will also try to find a no-load or low-load fund. *Load* is the word mutual funds use to refer to sales charges. Many advisors advocate that, whenever possible, you should choose a mutual fund that has no or low sales charges. All mutual funds are in business to make money, and they do so in many ways; some take the sales charges directly when you invest; others take out a sales charge when you redeem your shares. In addition, they all take some form of annual management fee. If you want the fund, you will have to pay the sales charge. As a rule, I try to avoid stock funds with annual expense ratios greater than 1.5 percent. You should also avoid funds that have total expense ratios greater than 5 percent. You can find sales charge information in the prospectus and annual report of the fund. The funds listed in Table 6.2 are all no-load mutual funds.

Opening a Mutual Fund Account

To review mutual funds, call the mutual fund's 800-number and request a prospectus and an annual report. It is wise to review two or three mutual

Table 6.2
Funds for Long-Term Investors

Funds	Styles	Objective	Minimum Investment ($)	Phone	Web Site
Funds That Invest in Large Companies					
ABN AMRO/Montag & Caldwell (Gro N)	LarGro	Growth	2,500	(800) 992-8151	www.abnamrofunds.com
Clipper	MidVal	Growth	5,000	(800) 776-5033	www.clipperfund.com
Dodge & Cox Stock	LarVal	Growth	2,500	(800) 621-3979	www.dodgeandcox.com
Excelsior Value & Restructuring	LarVal	Growth	500	(800) 446-1012	www.excelsiorfunds.com
Fidelity Dividend Growth	LarVal	Gro-Inc	2,500	(800) 544-8888	www.fidelity.com
Harbor Capital Appreciation	LarGro	Growth	1,000	(800) 422-1050	www.harborfund.com
Jensen Fund (Portfolio)	LarGro	Growth	1,000	(800) 992-4144	www.jenseninvestment.com
Oakmark (1)	MidVal	Growth	1,000	(800) 625-6275	www.oakmark.com
T. Rowe Price Blue Chip Growth	LarGro	Growth	2,500	(800) 225-5132	www.troweprice.com
Selected American Shares	LarVal	Gro-Inc	1,000	(800) 243-1575	www.selectedfunds.com
TCW (Galileo) Select Equity	LarGro	Growth	2,000	(800) 386-3829	www.tcwgroup.com
Thompson Plumb Growth	AllCap	Growth	1,000	(800) 999-0887	www.thompsonplumb.com
Funds That Invest in Mid-Size Companies					
Fidelity Value	MidVal	Growth	2,500	(800) 544-8888	www.fidelity.com
Homestead Value	MidVal	Gro-Inc	500	(800) 258-3030	www.homesteadfunds.com

(continued)

Table 6.2 *(Continued)*

Funds	Styles	Objective	Minimum Investment ($)	Phone	Web Site
Funds That Invest in Mid-Size Companies *(continued)*					
T. Rowe Price	Mid-cap	Growth	2,500	(800) 225-5132	www.troweprice.com
Strong Opportunity (Inv)	MidBlnd	Growth	2,500	(800) 368-3863	www.estrong.com
TCW Galileo Value Opportunities (1)	MidVal	Growth	25,000	(800) 386-3829	www.tcwgroup.com
Turner Mid-Cap Growth	MidGro	AggGro	2,500	(800) 224-6312	www.turner-invest.com
Vanguard Capital Opportunity	MidGro	AggGro	25,000	(800) 662-2739	www.vanguard.com
Vanguard Primecap	MidGro	AggGro	25,000	(800) 662-2739	www.vanguard.com
Funds That Invest in Small Companies					
ABN AMRO/Veredus Aggressive (Gro N)	SmlGro	AggGro	2,500	(800) 992-8151	www.abnamrofunds.com
Aegis Value	SmlVal	AggGro	10,000	(800) 528-3780	www.bgbinc.com
Buffalo Small-Cap	SmlBlnd	AggGro	2,500	(800) 492-8332	www.buffalofunds.com
FMI Focus (Fiduciary)	SmlGro	AggGro	1,000	(800) 811-5311	www.fiduciarymgt.com
Meridian Value	SmlVal	AggGro	1,000	(800) 466-6662	www.meridianfundsbvi.com
Needham Growth	SmlVal	AggGro	5,000	(800) 625-7071	www.needhamco.com
Royce Opportunity (Inv)	SmlVal	AggGro	2,000	(800) 221-4268	www.roycefunds.com
Royce Premier	SmlVal	AggGro	2,000	(800) 221-4268	www.roycefunds.com
RS Diversified Growth (A)	SmlVal	AggGro	5,000	(800) 766-3863	www.rsim.com

Funds That Invest in Companies of All Sizes

Fund			Min	Phone	Website
Brandywine	AllCap	AggGro	25,000	(800) 656-3017	www.bfunds.com
Gabelli Asset	AllCap	Growth	1,000	(800) 422-3554	www.gabelli.com
TIAA-Cref Equity Index	LarGro	Growth	1,500	(800) 223-1200	www.tiaa-cref.org
USAA Nasdaq 100 Index	LarGro	AggGro	3,000	(800) 531-8181	www.usaa.com
Vanguard 500 Miles (Inv)	LarBlnd	Gro-Inc	3,000	(800) 662-2739	www.vanguard.com
Vanguard Mid-Cap Index (Inv)	MidBlnd	AggGro	3,000	(800) 662-2739	www.vanguard.com
Vanguard Small-Cap Index Fund	SmlBlnd	AggGro	3,000	(800) 662-2739	www.vanguard.com
Vanguard Total International Stock	Diversified		3,000	(800) 662-2739	www.vanguard.com
Vanguard Total Stock Index	LrgBlnd	Gro-Inc	3,000	(800) 662-2739	www.vanguard.com
Waterhouse Dow 30	LrgVal		1,000	(800) 934-4448	www.tdwaterhouse.com

Sector Funds

Fund			Min	Phone	Website
American Gas Index (Rushmore)	Sector	Natl Rsc	2,500	(800) 343-3355	www.fbr.com
Firsthand Technology Value	Sector	Tech	10,000	(800) 884-2675	www.firsthandfunds.com
Third Avenue Real Estate	Sector	Realty	1,000	(800) 443-1021	www.vanguard.com
Vanguard Healthcare	Sector	Health	25,000	(800) 662-2739	www.vanguard.com
Vanguard Utilities Income	Sector	Utilities	3,000	(800) 662-2739	www.vanguard.com

(continued)

Table 6.2 *(Continued)*

Funds	Styles	Objective	Minimum Investment ($)	Phone	Web Site
Socially Screened Funds					
Ariel	SmlVal	AggGro	1,000	(800) 292-7435	www.arielmutualfunds.com
Ariel Appreciation	MidVal	Growth	1,000	(800) 292-7435	www.arielmutualfunds.com
Green Century Equity	LrgBlnd	Growth	2,000	(800) 934-7336	www.greencentury.com
Neuberger & Berman Socially Responsible	LrgVal	Growth	1,000	(800) 877-9700	www.nbfunds.com
Parnassus (Income Equity)	LarVal	AggGro	2,000	(800) 999-3505	www.parnassus.com
TIAA-Cref Social Choice Equity	MidVal	Growth	1,500	(800) 223-1200	www.tiaa-cref.org
(Vanguard) Calvert Social Index	LrgVal	Growth	3,000	(800) 662-2739	www.vanguard.com
Global Funds					
T. Rowe Price Global Stock	Global		2,500	(800) 225-5132	www.troweprice.com
Tweedy Browne Global Equity (Value)	Global		2,500	(800) 432-4789	www.tweedy.com
Foreign-Company Funds					
Artisan International	Diversified		1,000	(800) 344-1770	www.artisanfunds.com
Fidelity Diversified International	Diversified		2,500	(800) 544-8888	www.fidelity.com
Julius Baer International	Diversified		2,500	(800) 435-4659	www.juliusbaer.com
Longleaf Partners International	Diversified		10,000	(800) 445-9469	www.longleafpartners.com
Oakmark International	Diversified		1,000	(800) 625-6275	www.oakmark.com

Index Funds

Fund	Category	Style	Min	Phone	Website
TIAA-Cref Equity Index	LarGro	Growth	1,500	(800) 223-1200	www.tiaa-cref.org
USAA Nasdaq 100 Index	LarGro	AggGro	3,000	(800) 531-8181	www.usaa.com
Vanguard 500 Miles (Inv)	LarBlnd	Gro-Inc	3,000	(800) 662-2739	www.vanguard.com
Vanguard Mid-Cap Index (Inv)	MidBlnd	AggGro	3,000	(800) 662-2739	www.vanguard.com
Vanguard Small-Cap Index Fund	SmlBlnd	AggGro	3,000	(800) 662-2739	www.vanguard.com
Vanguard Total International Stock	Diversified		3,000	(800) 662-2739	www.vanguard.com
Vanguard Total Stock Index	LrgBlnd	Gro-Inc	3,000	(800) 662-2739	www.vanguarrd.com
Waterhouse Dow 30	LrgVal		1,000	(800) 934-4448	www.tdwaterhouse.com

High-Quality Corporate Bonds

Fund	Category	Min	Phone	Website
Fidelity Intermediate Bond	Int. Corp	2,500	(800) 544-8888	www.fidelity.com
Fremont Bond	Int. Corp	2,000	(800) 548-4539	www.fremontfunds.com
Harbor Bond	Int. Corp	1,000	(800) 422-1050	www.harborfund.com
Strong Advantage (Inv)	ST Corp	2,500	(800) 368-3863	www.estrong.com
Vanguard Long-Term Corporate	LT Corp	3,000	(800) 662-2739	www.vanguard.com
Vanguard Short-Term Corpo'ate	ST Corp	3,000	(800) 662-2739	www.vanguard.com
Vanguard Total (Market) Bond Index (Inv)	Int. Gov't	3,000	(800) 662-2739	www.vanguard.com

(continued)

Table 6.2 (Continued)

Funds	Styles	Objective	Minimum Investment ($)	Phone	Web Site
U.S. Treasury Bonds					
American Century Inflation-Adjusted Treasury	LT Gov't		2,500	(800) 345-2021	www.americancentury.com
Dreyfus U.S. Treasury Intermediate	Int. Gov't		2,500	(800) 645-6561	www.dreyfus.com
Vanguard Long-Term Treasury	LT Gov't		3,000	(800) 662-2739	www.vanguard.com
Vanguard Short-Term Federal	ST Gov't		3,000	(800) 662-2739	www.vanguard.com
Municipal Bonds					
Sit Tax-Free Income	LT Muni		5,000	(800) 332-5580	www.sitfunds.com
T. Rowe Price Tax-Free Income	LT Muni		2,500	(800) 225-5132	www.troweprice.com
USAA Tax-Exempt Intermediate	Int. Muni		3,000	(800) 531-8181	www.usaa.com
Vanguard Insured (Long-Term) Tax-Exempt	LT Muni		3,000	(800) 662-2739	www.vanguard.com
Vanguard Intermediate-Term Tax-Exempt	Int. Muni		3,000	(800) 662-2739	www.vanguard.com
Vanguard Limited Tax-Exempt	Int. Muni		3,000	(800) 662-2739	www.vanguard.com

Mortgage Securities

Fidelity (Advisor) Mortgage Securities (T)	Mort		2,500	(800) 622-3175	www.fidelity.com
Vanguard GNMA	Mort		3,000	(800) 662-2739	www.vanguard.com

High-Yield Corporate Bonds

Fidelity Capital & Income	HY Corp		2,500	(800) 544-8888	www.fidelity.com
Northeast Investors Trust	HY Corp		1,000	(800) 225-6704	www.northeastinvestors.com
Vanguard Short-Term Federal	ST Gov't		3,000	(800) 662-2739	www.vanguard.com

Funds That Invest in Companies of All Sizes

Brandywise	AllCap	Growth	25,000	(800) 656-3017	www.bfunds.com
Gabelli Assets	AllCap	Growth	1,000	(800) 422-3554	www.gabelli.com
Janus Mercury	AllCap	Growth	2,500	(800) 525-3713	www.janus.com
Legg Mason Opportunity (Pr mary)	AllCap	Growth	1,000	(800) 822-5544	www.leggmason.com
Olstein Financial Alert ©	AllCap	Growth	1,000	(800) 799-2113	www.olsteinfunds.com

(continued)

Table 6.2 *(Continued)*

Funds	Styles	Objective	Minimum Investment ($)	Phone	Web Site
Funds That Invest in Companies of All Sizes *(continued)*					
Weitz Partners Value	AllCap	Growth	25,000	(800) 232-4161	www.weitzfunds.com
Weitz Value	AllCap	Growth	25,000	(800) 232-4161	www.weitzfunds.com
Funds That Invest in Stocks and Bonds					
Dodge & Cox Balanced	Hybrid	Balanced	2,500	(800) 621-3979	www.dodgeandcox.com
Janus Balance	Hybrid	Balanced	2,500	(800) 525-3713	www.janus.com
Oakmark Equity & Income (I)	Hybrid	Gro-Inc	1,000	(800) 625-6275	www.oakmark.com
Strong Balance	Hybrid	Balanced	250	(800) 368-3863	www.estrong.com
Vanguard Wellesley Income	Hybrid	Gro-Inc	3,000	(800) 662-2739	www.vanguard.com
Vanguard Wellington (Inv)	Hybrid	Balanced	3,000	(800) 662-2739	www.vanguard.com

funds in a certain category. The best tool in the selection of a mutual fund is its prospectus. It provides all the information pertaining to a particular fund, including the fund's portfolio, investment objectives, manager, sales charges, expenses, history of past performance, number of shares issued, yields, and more. When reviewing the prospectus and annual report, look for answers to the following questions:

- What is the objective of the fund?
- What are the sales charges (loads)?
- Are there telephone exchange privileges? (Can you change your investment by phone?)
- Are reinvestments free? (Can you reinvest your dividends without charge?)
- Is the fund a member of a family of funds?
- What is the minimum initial investment?
- What is the fund's past performance? (Look at 1-, 3-, 5-, and 10-year returns.)
- How long must you stay in the fund to avoid back-end sale charges?
- What is the minimum IRA investment?
- Do they have a systematic bank withdrawal plan?

If you have questions after reading the prospectus and annual report, call the fund and ask an account service person for answers. If necessary, the service person also can recommend a local financial planner, broker, or registered representative who will review the prospectus with you. Again, your primary goal is to make sure that the mutual fund's investment objective matches your investment goal.

I highly recommend making regular investments directly through your employer, credit union, or bank. In general, many advisors suggest that investors have several mutual funds to achieve diversification. The best mutual funds are rated annually in several magazines and newspapers including *Money* magazine, *Kiplinger's Personal Finance, Barron's, Forbes,* and the *Wall Street Journal.*

These days, saving money for old age or even a rainy day is not a number one priority for a lot of young people. Too many have to worry about paying off immediate debts, and too many spend money needlessly. Couple that with now-famous Generation X apathy, and you can find a lot of not-so-smart money moves.

Millionaire in the Making

Erin, of Aurora, Colorado, is a testament to that. She said that she watched money fly out the window that she should have been spending elsewhere or saving. Those habits continued until her parents bought her a $22.50 ticket to a financial planning workshop run by a Denver-based financial planner, Rod Greiner. That experience changed her spendthrift attitude about money to frugality.

Now a program director at a Denver-area YMCA, Erin began to do simple things that she learned in the workshop. Instead of going out for lunch every day, she started brown-bagging it; instead of shopping regularly, she finds clearance sales to avoid paying full price; instead of seeing movies at prime time, she sees them during the twilight hours. These trends and others save her about $100 each month, $50 of which she invests in a money market fund. The fund yields her a rate that is about 2 percent to 3 percent better than most savings accounts these days. Much of the rest is invested through an investment bank. "I have a thing about debt," she says. "I don't like it." Erin said she initially wanted to have some emergency liquid money, but now she understands the security that comes with having a sound monetary status.

"Basically, my goal is just to live comfortably," she said. "If something happened to my job, I'd be able to make it through without debt." Once she reaches her objective of a $1,500 balance in her money market fund, she will begin to invest in stock funds for more lucrative growth. She says that the changes she has made are easy to do; they only require being in the right mind-set.

When investing in equity mutual funds, you need to give them a three- to five-year period to perform over an entire market cycle. The real discipline is to invest on a systematic basis over enough time for compound interest to increase the value of your portfolio. Your investment goal should be to get an annual return of 8 percent. A lot of pension funds try to average an annual 8 percent return.

Mutual funds will send you a prospectus to review before you open your account. Don't let the prospectus intimidate you. They read like legal documents because that is what they are. Mutual funds are highly regulated. Everything is laid out in the prospectus, but if you don't have a law degree, you may not feel comfortable going through every page. Mutual Fund manager Eugene Profit suggests that new mutual fund investors review several fund prospectuses and compare them. This activity he advises, "will help you see similarities among fund prospectuses and feel more comfortable with your mutual fund choice."

Often when you purchase a mutual fund from a financial representative, you will probably pay a sales fee to buy the fund. That is not necessarily all bad because that broker is going to educate you. You are really paying the financial representative to help you select an appropriate mutual fund.

If you don't like paying a sales fee, and many investors don't, then you can purchase your shares directly from the mutual fund company. Simply call the 800 number for one of the many no-load mutual funds and talk to their representatives. If the fund you are interested in has a local investor center near you, all the better. Go on in and sit down and talk with someone. Many times, these financial representatives are in a sense noncommissioned brokers and are on salary. Because all mutual funds have fees and they have already been taken into account, checking performance is what is really important—or you could end up choosing a low-fee mutual fund with poor performance.

The poet Melvin B. Tolson loved to recount how one day he came across a tumb stone which read; "I am dead as all can see. Prepare ye all to follow me." After reading these words, the young poet said to himself: "To follow you I'm not content. Until I know which way you went.

The poet's words shed light on the importance of the annual fund's past performance. You want to understand the direction your fund went in the past 3 years before you invest in it.

When reviewing the prospectus, look at the fund's returns for the past 5 to 10 years. This will help you determine whether the fund will fit your investment objectives. To learn more about your mutual fund, you can go online to Morningstar.com. Morningstar is highly regarded and is a reliable evaluator of mutual funds.

A word of caution concerning performance. Make sure that you are looking at the same category of mutual fund when you compare performance. You don't want to compare a large-cap stock fund with an international blue-chip fund. So if you're looking at a domestic blue-chip fund, compare its performance with other domestic blue-chip funds.

The Internet may be your best source of information about mutual funds. You can research and contact most mutual funds online. This fact notwithstanding, the best online web site to help fearful mutual fund investors become fearless is the Investment Company Institute web site (ICI.org is the Mutual Fund Trade Association's web site). At this site, you will find the *Investing for Success* program of the Investment Company Institute Education Foundation. This online investment resource center has it all. It explains how to set goals and start investing in funds, how to achieve diversification, and how to fund college educations and retirements. This unbiased web site has an entire set of tools with no sales literature and is great for timid investors.

Moneywise Master Class

Because mutual funds are so popular, they are often a topic of discussion on the *Moneywise* television series. During one such discussion, I was thrilled to have Denise Murray, the Director of Investor Awareness for the Investment Company Institute on the program. She appeared on the telecast when the stock market was down and many investors were afraid to open their quarterly statements. Her knowledge of the industry was and is comforting to many investors. Here is a portion of my interview with Denise Murray:

> **BOSTON:** Denise, what should people do now whose mutual funds are down in value?
>
> **MURRAY:** People shouldn't panic, and they should continue their investment program. Mutual fund investing is a long-term prospect. When the market or your mutual fund shares are low, I always tell people

that this is a great time to be in the market and a great time to be investing because you're buying shares at a lower price, so in the long term you'll see much more appreciation as the market and share value rise.

BOSTON: Any other advice for nervous stock investors?

MURRAY: Being an investor requires you to be diligent, and it requires you to be consistent. It is important when the market is down for people to just hold the course. As long as their investments and their mutual funds are matching their risks and their time horizons, they just need to continue and fight the good fight.

BOSTON: Now, let's talk a little bit about dollar cost averaging? Is this still the way most investors are going to make money in mutual funds?

MURRAY: Yes. Dollar cost averaging is a wonderful strategy because it allows you to invest in specific amounts every month. Take a monthly 401(k) contribution for example. Every month a certain amount of money will come out of your paycheck and be used to purchase shares of a mutual fund. The average means that your cost per share comes out to an average between buying at the highs and buying at the lows in the market. So it gives you the best opportunity to get price appreciation on your share. The other thing I'd like to add, though, is that I think one of the real benefits of dollar cost averaging is that it allows investors to get into a portfolio and put it almost on autopilot.

BOSTON: Are mutual funds just for the rich?

MURRAY: Mutual funds are for everyone, especially, I like to say, for beginning investors. An individual investor who doesn't have a lot of money could not purchase enough individual shares of stock to give them the diversification that's going to protect them from the volatility in the market. So mutual funds are great for people who have very little money. Some funds will allow you to invest at $50 a month.

BOSTON: Let's talk about pension plans and the role mutual funds play because, indeed, that's where many Americans are investing in mutual funds through their pension plans.

MURRAY: If their goal is long term, what they want to look at is the diversification within their portfolios. They shouldn't be too heavy in bonds. They should make sure that they are diversified among large company funds, small company funds, international and bond funds.

And oftentimes, pension plans will offer what is called a hybrid fund, and so that fund will automatically do the allocation. So if you're getting a hybrid fund it will have a certain amount in bonds and it will keep a certain amount in large companies and a certain amount in small companies, so that individuals don't actually have to select five or six different funds. They can select one fund that automatically gives them that diversification and that allocation.

BOSTON: Denise, what do you say to novice investors who are afraid of taking a risk with their money?

MURRAY: Many new investors tend to avoid risk. They like to think oh, I don't want to put my money in the market because, I might lose my money. But there are several types of risks and one of the risks is inflation risk. Let me use an example, many Americans will put that money in a savings account at the credit union. The credit union savings account may only be paying one percent interest. If inflation is two percent, it costs two percent more to buy goods. If your money is earning only one percent, then you're actually losing money. So there are several types of risks. The stock market's risk is often due to fluctuations. Studies show that with long-term investing many of the fluctuations associated with stock investments are diminished. This is why people must be patient or long-term investors. Slow and steady is the mantra of many successful mutual fund investors. Mutual funds are good vehicles to help people create wealth over time. And what I really want to do is to encourage more Americans to start thinking about creating wealth in the long term.

Murray's passion is to help people understand how they can use mutual funds (and other equity investments) to create wealth over time. She is passionate about this subject because she has seen it work for herself and the investors she serves at the Investment Company Institute. It can work for you, too. But you have to let it work for you.

People who are fearful of losing money in an investment like to say that "I can't lose what I don't invest." However, they also "can't share in the long-term appreciation of investments, if they don't invest." To win the prize, you have to get into the game. You must at least start investing in equities directly or indirctly, if you want to enjoy the wealth creation opportunity it can offer you over time.

Increasing your investment know-how will transform you from a fearful investor to a fearless investor. This may not happen overnight, but it will happen with time and patience. The information in this chapter can reduce your fear of making money-losing investment decisions and increase your ability to use equity mutual funds and investment clubs to increase your net worth. Now reflect on how you can use the information in this chapter to fund your financial dreams.

MASTER KEYS

Know

It is impossible to win the great prizes
of life without running risks.

—*Theodore Roosevelt*

Act

Join an investment club.
Visit the Investing for Success web site.
Use dollar cost averaging.
Start investing in mutual funds.
Keep learning about mutual funds.

Believe

I can become a confident investor.

7

SECURING YOUR RETIREMENT

Actually, I have no regard for money. Aside from its purchasing power, it's completely useless as far as I'm concerned.

—Alfred Hitchcock

EMOTIONAL FACTOR:
Fear of Growing Older

Every year, a national report (The Retirement Confident Survey from Employee Benefit Research Institute and America's Saving Education Council) is issued confirming that many Americans are just not saving for their retirement. In a culture based on self-directed retirement plans such as 401(k)s, now more than ever, Americans must plan for their future security.

Many of us know this, and many of us can afford to save for our retirement, but we fail to do so. Often, financial experts assume Americans won't save for their retirement for financial reasons. We all may be better served, however, if we start to consider the emotional reason Americans don't save for their retirement. Maybe, just maybe, many of us are afraid of growing old. Maybe many of us fear that we cannot afford to retire. These reasons may explain why we don't start saving until a few years before retirement age.

Planning how you are going to live during retirement is a wonderful experience. Let it be a time of joy and excitement and not a time to fear old age. The information in this chapter focuses on how you can start securing the retirement of your dreams.

Many people think that if they only had a higher income, all their financial problems would be solved. But that thinking can be an emotional financial trap. "What good is having a $500,000-a-year job if you are spending $500,001?" asks Larry Passaretti, a financial advisor with AXA in New York City and a member of the National Association of Insurance and Financial Advisors. "You'll be in the same place (maybe worse) than someone earning $40,000 a year." More important than income alone is saving and accumulating wealth, and that winning strategy is available at any income level.

Profile in Courage

Kristin, a personal coach, started her savings plan when she was 25. A single woman, she says that back then she had a "foggy notion" that security meant getting married, but figured she had better fend for herself, so she hired a financial advisor (with whom she still works) and set up a mutual fund account. When the opportunity presented itself, she invested in a 401(k) that she kept active for seven years. After she left that company and became self-employed, she rolled her fund into an IRA. She recently added a Roth IRA to her portfolio. Now at the age of 40, Kristin comments, "I am very glad I started my savings plan when I did," she says. "Though it's not much, it has made a huge difference in my feelings about my future."

While experts agree that it is best to start planning early, as Kristin did, it is never too late to start. "People who take control are going to be winners," says Passaretti. And the way to take control, no matter what your age, is through acquiring knowledge, developing winning strategies, and overcoming fear.

The Importance of Retirement Planning

Although you need to build up retirement assets as part of your comprehensive wealth-building strategy, this is the area that people most often overlook. They seem to believe that there will always be time or that there are more pressing expenses. If you change your thinking from "planning for retirement" to "planning for financial independence," you will open up doors to creating a retirement that is anything but retiring. According to John Sestina, financial planner and cofounder of the National Association of Personal Financial Advisors, "Almost anyone can be a millionaire, and that's not an exaggeration." It doesn't matter what your income is; what matters is your savings pattern. This is especially important in today's climate, where pension plans are becoming passé and the future of Social Security is fast becoming anything but secure.

Americans can no longer take a passive approach to the future. It behooves you instead to create your own safety net with several options for financial independence in those later years. And there is an incentive to start now. Thanks to compound interest and certain tax advantages, these assets will grow faster than other types of investments, allowing you to both secure your future and achieve your current million-dollar financial goals that much quicker.

How Assets Grow: Compound Interest, Tax Implications, Employer Match

The basic principle behind asset growth is compound interest. This simple principle applies to all savings plans. As the principal amount earns interest, that interest also starts earning interest, and on and on; it's an avalanche effect. At 4 percent interest compounded monthly over one year, $1,000 will become $1,041. Over 30 years, that same $1,000 will more than triple to $3,313. More good news is that the rate of return for longer-term assets is usually much higher. So, the same $1,000 that is only earning 4 percent in a short-term savings account could be earning 8 percent (or more) in a retirement account. Since your interest is earning higher interest and that higher interest is earning interest, doubling the interest rate does more than double your investment. That original $1,000 investment in 30 years would be a staggering $10,936 (see Table 7.1).

Table 7.1
The Power of Compound Interest—It All Starts with $1,000

Percent	1 Year Later ($)	10 Years Later ($)	20 Years Later ($)	30 Years Later ($)	40 Years Later ($)
3	1,030	1,349	1,821	2,457	3,315
4	1,041	1,491	2,223	3,313	4,940
6	1,062	1,819	3,310	6,023	10,957
8	1,083	2,220	4,927	10,936	24,273

In addition to compound interest, tax advantages are inherent in most retirement accounts. Employer-sponsored plans such as 401(k) plans use pretax dollars. Deductions are taken out of your paycheck before any taxes are calculated, resulting in less money being withheld. That translates into real dollars for you—immediately. More money goes into your retirement account than comes out of your paycheck. For a $500 increase in your retirement account, assuming a combined federal/state tax bracket of 38 percent, you will only feel an impact of $310 in your take-home pay. There is a similar benefit for nonemployer plans, such as IRAs. The Internal Revenue Code (IRC) contains a provision to allow a gross income deduction of $4,000 per year for each working person under 50 years of age. Assuming a federal tax bracket of 28 percent, this would cut a single person's tax bill by $1,260. You could also see a further savings on your state tax bill.

Employer-sponsored plans provide another key incentive: free money. The money I'm talking about is 401(k) matching contributions. A 401(k) is a retirement plan in which you and your employer work together to accumulate your wealth. The automatic payroll deductions that are taken out of your pretax earnings are usually matched 50 percent by your employer, up to a predetermined percentage (approximately 6 percent of your earnings, but it varies by employer). So, if you contribute $4,000 each year, your employer will kick in another $2,000. That is free money, on top of your regular salary.

Millionaire in the Making

Philip is a complex operations associate, and like Kristin, he started his savings plan early. The 27-year-old opened his 401(k) account 1½ years ago *when he began his current job. He has aggressive goals for the future, so he sets aside 10 percent of his salary, which is matched 50 percent by his employer. His account is valued at $7,500 and the current rate of return is 8.8 percent. Philip realizes that if he maintains his present participation level and rate of return, he will have $890,000 when he reaches 57—his target retirement age. But Philip isn't stopping there; he plans to regularly increase his contributions as his salary increases.*

Employer-Based and Nonemployer-Based Plans

The first step in starting a retirement savings plan is to look at what is available from your employer. As these plans generally offer matching contributions as an incentive to save, they are the most attractive option. If your employer doesn't offer such a plan, or if your savings goal exceeds the maximum allowable amount, don't worry—there are myriad savings plans out there. Almost all workers, even those who are self-employed, can take advantage of some type of retirement vehicle, from 401(k)s or 403(b)s to SEP (Simplified Employee Pension) IRAs or SIMPLE (Savings Incentive Match Plan for Employees) IRAs to deductible, nondeductible, or Roth IRAs, or a combination of these.

Details of Employer-Based Plans

What are 401(k) and 403(b) plans and how do they work? If offered by your company, employer-based plans are the easiest to enroll in. All you have to do is sign up, authorizing the payroll department to deduct a percentage of your wages (you determine that percentage) in pretax dollars and set them aside in a fund. You also choose where the funds are to be invested. Your payroll department will provide you with a menu of options, along with information such as the type of investment and past performance.

There are two small strings attached. To receive the employer match, you usually must stay with your employer for a certain period of time, typically one to three years, before becoming vested. But this only impacts the employer match; your contributions are yours to keep, no matter how long you stay with the company or why you leave. And if you leave before you reach 59½, vested or not, you can roll the balance of your account into another qualified retirement account. The other drawback is that you can't touch the money until you reach 59½. There are tax implications; if you draw the funds out early, the combined tax and penalty will end up costing you almost half of what you had saved. But this onerous penalty has one advantage. It helps you resist the temptation to dip into the fund, encouraging you to keep with your savings agenda.

The 401(k)s are primarily offered by large (over 100 employees) for-profit companies. Some employers who are unable to offer 401(k) plans offer 403(b) plans instead. From the employee's point of view, these plans, offered to employees of nonprofits, hospitals, schools, churches, and charities, function in much the same way as 401(k)s: Your contributions are handled by payroll deductions and are based on pretax earnings. You are not taxed on either your base deductions or your earnings until you withdraw the funds. The primary difference between 401(k)s and 403(b)s lies in your investment choices. With a 403(b), you are not limited to preselected choices. You are on your own in choosing where to invest your fund. This can be a boon to the fearless investor, or cause trepidation to those unfamiliar with the investment arena.

While the marketplace seems to offer a dizzying array of choices—you can't turn on the TV or open a magazine without seeing a dozen ads from companies wanting to handle your investment dollar—the two basic choices are mutual funds or annuity products. While annuity products (usually referred to as TSAs—tax-sheltered annuities) are the most prevalent, and therefore first on the radar screen for most 403(b) participants, they may not be the best choice for most investors. Resist the urge to make a choice based on a glossy ad or a sophisticated sales pitch. Instead, do your own research or get advice from a qualified, fee-based advisor. Most important, be wary of unsolicited agents. They work for a specific investment company and are not well-versed in the entire marketplace. Their interest is in their commission, not on whether the product they are selling is best suited to your needs.

There are also other retirement plans out there for small companies (those with 100 or less employees) and the self-employed. The SEP IRAs, SIMPLE IRAs, and Keoghs all offer some form of retirement savings, although their limits and rules vary. Most don't have the power of a 401(k), but if you work for a small company (or yourself), it behooves you to take advantage of these products, especially if they are the only option available to you. In a SEP IRA, employers determine how much per year they are willing to contribute, and everyone gets the same percentage of that pool based on his or her salary. If the company decides 5 percent will be allocated and your salary is $40,000, you will receive an allocation of $2,000. The major concern with this vehicle is that the contribution amount can vary from year to year, and in some years, an employer may decide not to contribute anything at all. You have very little control over your retirement planning if you rely solely on this vehicle. If you are eligible for a SIMPLE IRA, you can put in pretax earnings and your employer can decide whether to match those deductions (similar to a 401(k)) or to contribute an overall percentage to all employees (similar to a SEP IRA).

Both a SEP IRA and a SIMPLE IRA offer immediate vesting, an attractive option, especially if you plan on having a short-term relationship with your employer. A Keogh plan may have a vesting period, but what sets this plan apart is that it generally offers a higher contribution level. A Keogh plan is a defined contribution pension plan for self-employed individuals. Like an IRA the annual contributions are tax deductible and earnings are not taxed until the money is withdrawn, presumably in retirement. The limit is generally 25 percent of your self-employment earnings, to a maximum of $42,000 per year. Don't let the acronym *IRA* in some of these names confuse you. Yes, these are IRAs, but if you are participating in one of these three plans, you are still eligible to invest in a traditional or a Roth IRA. If you are participating in a 401(k) or a 403(b), you can also contribute to a traditional or a Roth IRA, but your tax benefit may be diminished.

Nonemployer-Based IRA Plans—Deductible, Nondeductible, Roth

IRAs can provide the same benefits as 401(k)s, but without the employer match component. IRA accounts can be opened at a bank, mutual fund company, or brokerage house, and can be started with a 401(k) rollover or simply by depositing cash. The trick is to choose the account that is best suited to your needs. A bank IRA is most commonly CD-based, with rates that increase with the length of the term. These rates are conservative and remain fixed regardless of rate fluctuations in the marketplace. For example, you can purchase a CD-based IRA at your local bank for a five-year term at 4.6 percent at the time of this writing. The same type of CD may be offered six months or one year later with a different rate—higher or lower—but your rate will remain unchanged. If you decide to either liquidate or transfer the fund before the term ends, the bank will impose a penalty—typically a portion of interest earned. Most have automatic rollover features; the bank will notify you when the account is about to mature. If you do not react, the account will roll over and the term will restart at the most current rate.

These accounts are best if you are dealing with a short-term decision such as rolling over a 401(k), or making a deliberately conservative investment choice. However, because these are by nature short-term investments, the rates are low.

Your best option, especially if you are years away from retirement, may be to open an IRA at a brokerage house and invest your savings in the various choices, including stocks and bonds, that they offer. There are limitations to the contribution level and the immediate tax benefits of an IRA. Your annual contribution is limited to $4,000, and your maximum deduction is also $4,000 (for single filers), and $8,000 for couples. If you already are investing in a 401(k), you may not be eligible to take a deduction on your taxes. But even if your immediate tax benefits are limited, your earnings will still grow, tax free. You will not be taxed on any earnings until you take the money out.

Another IRA option is the Roth IRA. Under the terms of a Roth IRA, there are no immediate tax benefits—you cannot take an IRA deduction on your tax return (although you are still subject to the contribution limit previously discussed). So, what's the appeal? The Roth IRA provides more flexibility in your future tax planning. With a Roth IRA, you pay tax on your contributions now, so that when you draw on the funds postretirement, the distributions are tax free. According to Jamie Richardson, a financial planner in Texas, when thinking about investing in a Roth IRA, you should look at your tax bracket now and what you expect it to be during retirement. If you have a mix of tax-free and taxable income streams, you can alleviate a tax burden in your later years. Like a traditional IRA, your earnings grow tax free. These earnings also remain tax free on distribution.

Best Mix

When choosing where to deposit your retirement funds, the first choice by far is a plan with an employer match, if one is available. Take the max on the 401(k) even if it is above your target savings goal. Quite simply, there is never a good reason to turn away free money. This will also allow you a cushion if you don't have this option later in your career. If you are making the maximum allowable contribution to your 401(k) and still have not met your goal, supplement your savings with an IRA. A factor to keep in mind is the distribution you will have when you retire. For people just starting out, putting a large percentage or all of their money in a tax-deferred vehicle makes the most sense. However, you may want to set some funds aside in a Roth IRA, especially if your savings plan is aggressive and you are exceeding the IRS deduction limit for an IRA (but are still within the contribution limit).

Fear of locking up funds for a seemingly far-off event is the big reason most people avoid taking advantage of retirement plans. That fear can manifest itself as procrastination—a feeling that saving for retirement can wait for another day. There's always tomorrow. But consider this: compound interest works in your favor more so when you give it enough time. And there is a huge difference in the 10 years between a 30-year window and a 40-year window. If you are intent on retiring comfortably when you are 65, the best time to start planning is when you are 25 (see Table 7.2).

Logic notwithstanding, when it comes to locking money into a retirement account, the question that always gets raised is, "What if I need the money?" Sestina says that is the whole point. The best thing that you can do is put your savings in a place where it is not easily accessible. You will quickly discover that when you can't readily tap into it, you can get by without it. Remember Philip? He says that he likes his money and wants to keep as much of it as he can. He has discovered that having his funds locked into a 401(k) helps him to not spend his money on things that he really doesn't need or that will be used or gone in six months. This inaccessibility is a wonderful cure for "leakage": If your savings are too easy to dip into, you

Table 7.2
Yield of 401(k) at Age 65

Annual Contribution ($)	How Much Will I Have at Age 65 if I Start a 401(k) at		
	25 Years Old ($)	35 Years Old ($)	45 Years Old ($)
2,000	872,752	372,590	147,255
3,000	1,309,128	558,885	220,883
4,000	1,745,504	745,180	294,510

Note: All calculations are based on a rate of 8%.

may be tempted to splurge after you get to a certain level. Having your savings in an inaccessible place will help you avoid temptation. If there is a true emergency, a 401(k) offers a relief valve. You can take loans against the fund and you can even liquidate the account, but both options are like the cigarette in the glass case. Knowing it is there helps, but who wants to clean up the broken glass? These options should generally be avoided, because they will cost you. A loan against your 401(k) will impede the earnings growth. And liquidating your 401(k) will cost you in terms of the 10 percent tax penalty that the IRS imposes on top of the tax on the distribution. This may not seem like much, but do the math. A $5,000 liquidation will cost you a tax payment of $1,900 in regular taxes (assuming a 38 percent tax bracket) plus a $500 penalty. That is a whopping $2,400 tax bill at the end of the year, so you lose a $5,000 asset for spending power of only $2,600—roughly half the amount you withdrew.

Case Study

Cinnamon is employed by the Springfield, Massachusetts, school department. Her husband is employed at the local hospital. They each have a 403(b) and take advantage of the maximum participation amount primarily for tax purposes. Hit with a $5,000 tax bill four years ago, they discovered that raising their participation amount reduces their taxes, and allows them to save more money.

Developing Goals: How Much to Invest

When it comes to taking advantage of your employer match, the quick answer is to invest the maximum amount that your employer will match. If you are earning $40,000 and the max is 6 percent, $3,600 will be deposited into your account each year. But that is just a starting point. Don't be lulled into thinking that "maximum" means best for you. Most plans will allow you to put in more, usually up to about 10 percent. You won't have the benefit of the additional matching funds, but you will still maintain the tax advantages and the compound earnings. But will that be enough? What is enough? Most people don't like this question. According to Richardson, most people spend more time planning the family vacation than they do their retirement. If you think about it, figuring out your long-term goals is more critical than which beach to visit, yet still, vacation planning usually takes top priority.

If you have already taken the important first step of starting a savings plan, then you need to go all the way and make sure that it is sufficient for your needs. Determining how much to set aside now should not be a function of your current earnings, but rather of your future expectations. Figuring out what these expectations are and how much you should put aside is more than a matter of deciding when you want to retire. According to Richardson, you need an integrated strategy. To develop that strategy, you need to answer a different question. The three-part question, according to Sestina, should be: When do you want to become financially independent; what does that mean to you; and how much will you need to meet those objectives? Where are you going and what's enough to do what you want to do? That takes a proactive approach that can't be solved by simply saving what's left over, if anything, at the end of the month and hoping for the best. The good news is that answering these questions can be a lot more exciting than just deciding when you want to stop working. Not too long ago, answers to these questions were easier. For our grandparents, retirement meant working until 65 and then simply not working, whether they liked it or not. Life expectancy was also shorter, so retirement funds didn't have to be stretched as far. But this isn't your grandparents' retirement. These days, retirement can mean a lot more than stopping work. For some, it means starting a new career, spending time with family, or traveling the world. When do you want to do these things? For some it can be earlier, but for others, it may be later. If you are happy with your career and can't see yourself not working, then why stop?

The next question to ask is how much you will need to maintain the lifestyle you envision. Can you get by on $2,000 a month, or $4,000? A starting estimate is generally 70 to 80 percent of your current living expenses. If you plan on doing a lot of travel, however, your new lifestyle may have a heftier price tag, and you must factor in those costs. Likewise, if your postretirement plans include working, maybe teaching part-time at the local community college, you can expect to be earning some income. This can also be factored in. Putting a dollar sign on your dreams can be difficult. It is easy to be overly optimistic when making long-range decisions. According to

Passaretti, financial planners can keep you on track. They can acid-test your goals and help you determine whether they are feasible. They can provide an objective, fact-based analysis of the costs for your dreams. Most important, they can help you figure out what you need to do now to make those dreams happen.

"Most people just don't save enough. They don't know what they need. They have a big gap between what they need and their income," says Richardson. One of the biggest problems that all financial planners see in their postretirement clients is that they are outliving their assets. If you plan on retiring at 55, you will need to plan for 45 years—a period longer than your actual working life. Otherwise, you may have to take a part-time job to supplement your savings. Nothing can be more devastating than to dream of traveling the world and instead find yourself working part-time at Circuit City. You also should consider contingencies. What about long-term health care and other emergencies? These costs can sap your savings.

How do you translate all this information into a savings plan? There are several retirement calculators online. If you do a Google search for "retirement calculators" you will find a list, including ones at Vanguard.com and Bloomberg.com. These will help you figure out how to turn that amorphous future sum into an annual target.

Getting a Ballpark Estimate

One of the best online retirement calculators is the Ballpark E\$timate® produced by the Employee Benefit Research Institute's® (EBRI®'s) Education and Research Fund. This calculator will help you understand how much to save each month to reach your retirement goal. If the figure appears to be more than you can afford to put away, don't be discouraged; use these figures to motivate you to start saving more for your retirement. Form 7.1 is a basic version of this retirement calculator. You can complete this estimate in a few minutes. You can learn more about the Ballpark E\$timate® and fill out a longer version online by visiting Choosetosave.org. The basic aim of this calculator is to show you roughly how much you need to save now to secure your retirement later in life.

Form 7.1 simplifies several retirement planning issues such as projected Social Security benefits and earnings assumptions. It reflects today's dollars;

Form 7.1
Get a Ballpark Estimate of Your Retirement Needs

The ChoosetoSave.org and American Savings Education Council's
Planning and Saving Tool

Planning for retirement is not a one-size-fits-all exercise. The purpose of Ballpark is simply to give you a basic idea of the savings you need to set aside today for when you plan to retire.

If you are married, you and your spouse should each fill out your own Ballpark Estimate worksheet taking your marital status into account when entering your Social Security benefit in number 2 below.

1. How much annual income will you want in retirement? (Figure at least 70% of your current annual gross income just to maintain your current standard of living; however, you may want to enter a larger number. See the tips below.) $ _____

   Tips to help you select the goal:

70% to 80%—You will need to pay for the basics in retirement, but you won't have to pay many medical expenses as your employer pays the Medicare Part B and D premium and provides employer-paid retiree health insurance. You're planning for a comfortable retirement without much travel. You are older, and/or in your prime earning years.

80% to 90%—You will need to pay your Medicare part B and D premiums and pay for insurance to cover medical costs above Medicare, which on average covers about 55%. You plan to take some small trips, and you know that you will need to continue saving some money.

100% to 120%—You will need to cover all Medicare and other health-care costs. You are very young and/or your prime earning years are ahead of you. You would like a retirement lifestyle that is more than comfortable. You need to save for the possibility of long-term care.

2. Subtract the income you expect to receive annually from:

   • Social Security—If you make under $25,000, enter $8,000; between $25,000–$40,000, enter $12,000; over $40,000, enter $14,500. (For married couples—the lower earning spouse should enter either their own benefit based on their income or 50% of the higher earnings spouse's benefit, whichever is higher.)   – $ _____

   • Traditional Employer Pension—a plan that pays a set dollar amount for life, where the dollar amount depends on salary and years of service (in today's dollars)   – $ _____

   • Part-time income   – $ _____

   • Other (reverse annuity mortgage payments, earnings on assets, etc.)   – $ _____

   This is how much you need to make up for each retirement year: = $ _____

(continued)

Form 7.1 *(Continued)*

Now you want a Ballpark Estimate of how much money you'll need in the bank the day you retire. For the record, we assume you'll realize a constant real rate of return of 3% after inflation and you'll begin to receive income from Social Security at age 65.

3. To determine the amount you'll need to save, multiply the amount you need to make up by the factor below.

Choose your factor based on life expectancy (at age 65):

Female, 75th Percentile (age 92)

Male, 90th Percentile (age 94)

Female, 90th Percentile (age 97)

55	18.79	20.53	21.71	22.79	23.46	24.40
60	16.31	18.32	19.68	20.93	21.71	22.79
65	13.45	15.77	17.35	18.79	19.68	20.93
70	10.15	12.83	14.65	16.31	17.35	18.79

$ _____

4. **If you expect to retire before age 65,** multiply your Social Security benefit from line 2 by the factor below.

Age you expect to retire: 55   Your factor is: 8.8
                           60   4.7

+ $ _____

5. Multiply your savings to date by the factor below (include money accumulated in a 401(k), IRA, or similar retirement plan).

If you plan to retire in: 10 years   Your factor is: 1.3

                             15 years   1.6

                             20 years   1.8

                             25 years   2.1

                             30 years   2.4

                             35 years   2.8

                             40 years   3.3

− $ _____

Total additional savings needed at retirement: = $ _____

Don't panic. We devised another formula to show you how much to save each year to reach your goal amount. This factors in compounding. That's where your money not only makes interest, your interest starts making interest as well, creating a snowball effect.

Form 7.1 *(Continued)*

6. To determine the ANNUAL amount you'll need to save, multiply the TOTAL amount by the factor below.

If you want to retire in:		Your factor is:	
	10 years		.085
	15 years		.052
	20 years		.036
	25 years		.027
	30 years		.020
	35 years		.016
	40 years		.013

= $ _____

Reprinted with permission from EBRI.

therefore, you need to recalculate your retirement needs annually and as your salary and circumstances change.

It also assumes that your wages will increase at the same rate as inflation. This compares with the 2005 intermediate assumptions by the Social Security trustees that wages will increase 1.1 percent faster than inflation. When wage growth is larger than the inflation rate, this situation often requires a higher rate of savings than this worksheet suggests. A paper worksheet using an example where wage growth is not equal to inflation would be much more complicated.

Should you want a ballpark estimate that allows you to assume a wage growth that is different from the rate of inflation, you need to use the interactive ballpark estimate worksheet at http://www.choosetosave.org/ballpark.

The mission of the American Savings Education Council (ASEC) is to make savings retirement planning a priority for all Americans. American Savings Education Council is a program of the Employee Benefit Research Institute's Education and Research Fund. For information on becoming an ASEC Partner, visit www.asec.org.

With an annual target, you turn your long-term goal into a short-term goal; you can chart your progress and achieve immediate results. By focusing on your retirement needs as a current, wealth-building goal, you are on your way to success (see Table 7.3).

Table 7.3

Annual Contribution Required Based on Target Goal at 8 Percent

Target ($)	IRA			401(k)		
	20 Years ($)	30 Years ($)	40 Years ($)	20 Years ($)	30 Years ($)	40 Years ($)
500,000	10,250*	4,000	1,725	6,800	2,700	1,150
750,000	15,250*	6,000*	2,600	10,200	4,000	1,725
1,000,000	20,400*	8,100*	3,450	13,600	5,375	2,300

*Requires IRA plus after-tax vehicle (exceeds IRS contribution limit).

Tips on Meeting Goals

Now that you have figured out how much money to set aside, you need to come up with a practical strategy. The best way to do that is to first break down your annual savings goal into a more manageable monthly goal. For example, instead of thinking about saving $4,000 a year, shoot for $334 per month. It already seems more manageable, doesn't it? The best way to ensure success in meeting your savings goal is to change how you think about it. Instead of treating it like a chore or an obligation, you need to change your lifestyle. But the good news is that, with a little discipline, you can make your savings plan a simple force of habit. The first step is to treat yourself like a corporation. That's right, imagine that you are the [your name] Corporation, and you are the CEO. One of the perks of the job is that you pay yourself first. Before the mortgage or the car payment, or even before the Visa bill, you get paid. If you are paying into an employer-sponsored plan, that payment will happen automatically through payroll deductions once you enroll. If not, the first check that you write every payday needs to be to you and deposited immediately into your retirement account. Some employers allow direct deposits to be split into two accounts. If you have this option, use it.

Along with the perks of your new job title, come some responsibilities. The primary ones are budgeting and expense analysis. Just as every CEO knows where the money is going, you must know as well. How much is your monthly mortgage or rent payment? How about utilities? Look at how much you are realistically paying for things like your children's school tuition and fees. Most of these costs are fairly fixed, so they are easy to plan for. But other costs, such as food, clothes, and entertainment, are more flexible and can easily get away from you if you don't keep track. This is where the expense analysis comes in. Start keeping an expense diary and look at where the money goes each month. You could be in for a surprise. Once you know where the money goes, you can start a program of spending smart. Look at your monthly expenses and figure out where the waste is. You should scrutinize any expenditures that aren't building assets, no matter how necessary you think they are. According to Richardson, look hard at cash flow. "How is money being spent? Do you really need a new car? What about restaurant spending?" Are you making lifestyle choices that are sapping your cash flow? Do you eat out often just to avoid cooking? Do you drive to work, incurring gas, parking, and automobile wear and tear, when there are public transportation options? Lifestyle choices need to be conscientious decisions. Make educated choices and realize what these conveniences are actually costing you. It is not just the larger, more obvious choices that need scrutiny.

When you are looking at your spending patterns, avoid lumping expenses into categories that are too broad because the smaller, incidental expenses could also trip you up. Do you stop for a cup of gourmet coffee on your way into work? A lot of people claim that they can't survive without that morning cup of Joe, but once you look at your expenses, you may realize that you can't survive with it. There is an almost insidious difference between the cost of fancy, coffeehouse coffee and home-brewed Folgers or Maxwell House. It may seem like a minor luxury—after all, how much damage can a $3.50 small latte do to your budget? Well, if you do the math, that $3.50 Monday through Friday comes to $17.50 a week or $910 a year. And we know from our discussion on compound interest, that that $910 could be part of a wealth-building asset, quietly multiplying. One year's worth of coffee, $910, at 8 percent over 40 years is $22,089. That's just for the small size! If that's not enough to kick the habit, then consider this: Spending $3.50 a day over 40 years will end up costing you $264,735. Next time you are waiting in line for a latte, think about what you could do with a check for $265,000.

How many other minor luxuries are in your routine expenses? Smart lifestyle changes based on more efficient spending can possibly net you your entire savings goal. Paying yourself first and creating a budget to live within these new constraints involves a reversal of patterns. But it is also a question of balance. "It's not about 'no, no, no'" according to Sestina. "If you make sacrifices now, you can ease up later. Planning is about figuring out what you can do now to make it easier on yourself later." It is a simple matter of delayed gratification. If you simply can't break the Starbucks habit, put a line item in your budget, say $10 per month, and when that is spent, no more Starbucks until next month. It may be tough at first, but with a little discipline at the start, it will get easier. You may eventually find that you can take the $10 out altogether. A realistic budget that includes all your routine expenses is easier to manage and follow. This isn't a one-time task; regularly review your expenses. It should become an exercise in priorities. As you look at your spending habits in black and white and compare this activity with your long-term goals, you can gauge your spending by what is truly important: your million-dollar goal. Do you really need to eat out twice a week, or is that an excess that you can cut back on? Like any wise CEO, you should always look for ways to improve spending efficiencies and cut back on waste.

Where to Invest (Implementing Strategies)

Once a builder decides to build a house, he doesn't just go out to an empty lot with a pile of bricks and start building. He needs a plan—a blueprint—and an architect to guide him. He also needs tools such as a level, so that he can periodically check to see how he's doing. He needs to make sure that his corners are square and that the construction standards are meeting his expectations. His hard work pays off when the house he envisioned becomes a reality. Just like that builder, you need a blueprint and you need to periodically check your progress to make sure you are true to your goals.

Portfolio Allocation

To maximize your investment, you need to pay attention to how your investment is managed. If you are investing in a 401(k), your employer will most likely hand you a ridiculously long list of investment options. And if you are investing in an alternate vehicle (such as a 403(b) or an IRA), you have seemingly infinite choices. It is all too easy to be overwhelmed. But while it may seem that all investment options are created equal or that your fledgling portfolio is too small to make a difference, resist the urge to just pick one and be done with it. It really does matter. Your best course of action is to sit down with a financial planner to determine which investment option is best suited to your particular situation. Even if you are investing in a 401(k) and are choosing from a menu provided by your employer, it may be to your advantage to have someone help you make sense of it all. (Just make sure that you talk to a fee-based financial planner—someone who works for you and will give you advice best suited to your needs.) While right now, the fund may not seem significant enough to warrant professional advice, the growth factor of compound interest means that a 1 percent or 2 percent difference in rates of return over 30 years can make a substantial difference in results (see Table 7.4).

Smart planning now can result in faster asset growth. With or without a financial planner, you need some basic rules to guide you in making your investment choices. The two key principles to keep in mind are capacity for risk and diversification. A fee-based financial planner will work with you to put together an asset allocation model, basically a template—or blueprint—of the different investment products (stocks, bonds, mutual funds, etc.) best suited to both your capacity for risk and your age (how long-range your investment will be). Risk tolerance is a very individual trait; it is also a function of the time span of your investment. The stock market can provide greater overall growth, if you have the time and the stamina. Some people are willing to ride the waves of the stock market, where the potential for earnings is highest, but the potential for losses is also greater. People in their 20s can withstand more risk and experience greater overall growth in the stock market than investors in their 50s. So an asset allocation for those in their 20s can safely be more heavily weighted in stocks than in bonds. A

Table 7.4
What Difference Does a Percent or Two Make?
Yields from Investing $3,500 per Year in an IRA

Percent	10 Years ($)	20 Years ($)	30 Years ($)	40 Years ($)
4	42,948	106,976	202,431	344,739
6	47,798	134,762	292,984	580,851
8	53,359	171,798	434,688	1,018,211

proper allocation should also be diversified, with your portfolio spread out over a variety of investments.

The principle here is that a downturn in one investment can be recouped by an upturn in another. This is the same principle that makes money market funds an attractive investment. A good rule of thumb is to have no more than 20 percent of your assets tied up in one company including your own employer. One of your 401(k) investment options is always company stock, and some companies provide other incentives for their employees to own their stock. As a result, your sense of loyalty may compel you to weight your 401(k) heavily in your own company's stock. Here is where the principle of diversification is significant. Especially if you are already participating in a stock purchase plan or have other holdings tied up in your company's performance, resist the urge to tie your retirement investment to the growth of your employer. Your income is also tied to your company's performance, so limit these holdings.

Reviewing Goals and Strategies

A retirement blueprint should be a fluid tool, flexible to life's changes. So as your goals change or as your life changes, perhaps through marriage or divorce, reassess your long-term goals to determine whether they still are relevant. And with every goal change, do what Passaretti suggests and acid-test your decisions. In addition to reevaluating goals, you should also regularly look at how your funds are invested. "People buy things on yesterday's news—they base decisions on what happened in the market last year." According to Passaretti, it pays to be forward thinking. "You need to invest in where the market is going, not where it was." This yearly review of your fund should include how much you put aside (compared with your target), how much you earned, and how much you saved in taxes. This review will provide you with positive reinforcement because you can see that every year brings you one step closer to your goal.

Changing Jobs

One of the often-overlooked challenges with employer-based plans is that they are tied to your time at your job. There are a few potential minefields. Two of these are related to decisions you may make about leaving your company. One is the timing of switching jobs before you are vested; the other is switching jobs to a company that does not offer a similar retirement plan. If you decide to leave your company, make sure that you know when you will be vested in your company's plan, assuming you aren't already. If you are only one month away, it would behoove you to prolong your departure date to get the matching funds that have been accruing in your plan. If the vesting date is some distance away and your new opportunity offers significant advantages, by all means, forgo the funds. Where you are in the vesting process should be a part of your overall decision-making process.

Another consideration when deciding to switch jobs is a comparison of retirement plans. Not all plans are created equal. Analyze the two plans as carefully as you analyze the pros and cons of job duties, salary, commute, and other factors. Once you decide to leave your company, you must be ready to answer the question of what to do with your 401(k) or other employer-based retirement account. This pitfall thwarts the saving goals of many people. You get that letter asking what you want to do with your savings. If you are switching to a company that offers a 401(k) plan, you can easily roll your existing account into the new one without incurring any penalty. When that is not an option, you can roll the account into an IRA plan.

If you don't already have an IRA account, you may feel that—in the midst of all the other turmoil surrounding your job change—that this is one decision you aren't motivated to make. Resist the option to just pocket the money and start over, even if the amount seems small. Choosing to dissolve an account when switching jobs is the biggest mistake people make. When you look at the math, you can see why. Suppose you are faced with a distribution of $3,000. If you decide to just take the money, you must pay taxes on that money in the current year along with the 10 percent tax penalty, as discussed earlier. That may not seem like much, but that $3,000 will be worth a significant amount more if you roll it over into another qualified retirement account. At 8 percent, in 30 years that $3,000 could be worth $32,807. Are you willing to give up $33,000 for a current spending spree of $1,560?

Thinking of an IRA as "locking up your money" is problematic and can lead you to make unsound decisions. By now you know the real power behind retirement accounts: It's all in the math. Retirement accounts such as

401(k)s and IRAs allow you to build up an asset base a lot quicker than other, after-tax, methods. The money you are setting aside is only a small portion of the resulting asset size (see Table 7.5).

Securing your retirement will become a moot point if you do not save. Many Americans are not saving anything toward their retirement. LeCount Davis, a Certified Financial Planner (CFP) and Principal at LRD Management Group, notes, "A lot of clients say I can't afford to put money into my 401(k) or into any other retirement plan because I'm spending more than I'm making. Even when their contributions are matched by the employer they're still not putting the money in their plans." Davis helps these clients by showing them how to live within their means and helping them find a few extra dollars each month they can save in their company's retirement plan. He often states, "We have to start with the basics and the basics are spend less, save more."

If you cannot contribute the maximum in your 401(k) or pension plan, contribute as much as you can annually. To remind you to do so remember the advice a judge offered a man he had just sentenced.

A 50 year old man had committed a terrible crime. So the judge sentenced him to 50 years in jail. when hearing his sentence, the man pleaded to the judge. "Your honor I cannot do 50 years." To which the judge replied, "Well just do the best you can!"

If you cannot contribute the annual maximum to your pension plan, just do the best you can. But make it a point to save annually in your pension account.

Beth Hirschhorn, a marketing officer of MetLife Insurance Company believes that this advice is especially important for consumers who want to se-

Table 7.5
Comparison of Earnings versus Cash Outflow

Annual Contribution ($)	IRA			401(k)		
	Account Value ($)	Cash Outflow ($)	Pure Gain ($)	Account Value ($)	Cash Outflow ($)	Pure Gain ($)
2,000	581,835	57,600	524,235	872,752	57,600	815,152
3,000	872,752	86,400	786,352	1,309,128	86,400	1,222,728
4,000	1,163,669	115,200	1,048,469	1,745,504	115,200	1,630,304

Note: Assumes 8 percent over 40 years and tax savings of 28 percent.

cure their retirement. She indicates that studies often show, "There is a lot of misconceptions about retirement and key risks facing people in retirement. People greatly underestimate how long they're going to live. They greatly underestimate how much they'll need in retirement, and they overestimate how much they can spend, the rate at which they can spend down their retirement money."

Moneywise Master Class

Many Americans fear the United States may have to cope with a retirement crisis due to the estimated 70 million baby boomers who may retire in the next 20 years, the rising cost of health care, and the prospect that our Social Security system will one day go bankrupt. John Rother, Director of Policy and Strategy at AARP, appeared on *Moneywise* to answer these and other retirement-related questions. Here is a portion of my interview with John Rother:

BOSTON: John, are we facing a retirement crisis?

ROTHER: Millions of Americans are facing a crisis because they're at risk now under the new types of retirement plans. Second, millions of Americans have not saved adequately. And then third, we're looking at health care costs still increasing twice the level of inflation. Twenty years into retirement that's going to be a big expense item. The longer you live the more health care is going to cost, and most Americans are not ready for that.

BOSTON: You mentioned new types of retirement plans, what do you mean?

ROTHER: Under the old system the employer guaranteed you a certain retirement benefit that you knew you could count on like Social Security. Under the new plans, like 401(k) plans, you have put away a certain amount of money but your monthly retirement benefit will depend on the market ups and downs.

BOSTON: How much savings do people need to retire?

ROTHER: Well many retirees today are living on 50 percent of what they had when they were working but you know that's because they're not paying a mortgage and their health costs are covered. I think if you're facing debt, if you're facing paying out of pocket for health care you really should shoot much more toward the 70 or 75 percent of your income.

BOSTON: John, your organization works for a lot of retirees. What helps retirees feel successful?

ROTHER: Well you know I think part of it is the money. But a bigger part frankly is having something you like to do in retirement and thinking of it almost as a second career. Or something that really motivates you to get out of bed every morning. For some people, it's giving back to the community and being a volunteer, for other people its travel, for other people it's starting their own business. So a successful retirement isn't just stopping doing something else; its moving to another stage of your life and really embracing that and investing in yourself.

BOSTON: Should you max out your 401(k) and IRA?

ROTHER: I believe in maxing out of all of them, there's tax benefits involved.

BOSTON: John, are there other concerns people in this age group should understand?

ROTHER: I find that the two biggest mistakes that people make in their forties are number one they don't pay attention to their health coverage and then if they have a big health problem and they have to pay a huge amount of money, that can wipe them out. The biggest cause of bankruptcies in the United States today is health care. And number two they make the mistake of taking the retirement money out in order to do something else and then they never catch up.

BOSTON: Let's talk about someone who is maybe fifty years old and then someone who has already retired.

ROTHER: Well at fifty hopefully you've figured out how to get your kids educated and its time to really get serious about a retirement plan. What we find is a lot people don't really pay attention to retirement until they turn fifty. And then they have maybe ten or fifteen years, not a lot of time, but enough time if they're very disciplined and if they do have a plan. So I think that's the time that people end up going to a professional or maybe a web site to get more information and I think the more information the better at that point.

Boston: And suppose I'm retired, do I stop saving for my retirement when I hit sixty-five?

Rother: One other big mistake that we find people make is they retire in their late fifties based on the next year's spending requirements, oh I've got it covered I can retire. They're not thinking twenty years down the road and that's a big mistake. Having a plan that projects expenses way into the future is really important.

Boston: Many financial advisors believe that annuities are going to help Americans secure their retirement. John, what is an annuity and how can it help people plan for their retirement?

Rother: An annuity is an insurance product that you can purchase with a lump sum that gives you a lifetime monthly income. You can't outlive an annuity. So it's a way of dealing with the risk that you might live a very long time.

Many people are not saving for their retirement because they are afraid that they cannot afford to do so. Others feel that even if they do save, they still won't have enough to secure the retirement they desire. These individuals often feel as if they are in a no-win situation. But this is not the case. Most working Americans can secure the money they need for their retirement. To do so, you must remember that even a small retirement savings account is better than no retirement savings account. More important, every dollar put toward your retirement counts—sometimes two times, when matched by your employer. Take a few minutes to consider how you can secure your retirement.

MASTER KEYS

Know

None will improve your lot, if you yourself do not.

—*Bertolt Brecht*

Act

It is never too early or too late to save for your retirement.
Have a retirement plan.
Remember life doesn't end with retirement.
Find something you love to do during retirement.
Max out your retirement plans.
Have a ballpark estimate of your savings needs.

Believe

I can and will enjoy the retirement of my dreams.

8

INSURING YOUR FINANCIAL DREAMS

It ain't over till it's over.

—*Yogi Berra*

EMOTIONAL FACTOR:
Fear of Discussing Mortality

This chapter explores how to insure your income and overcome your fear of discussing mortality. Because we are humans, we may become disabled and we will eventually pass away. Understandably, many people feel uncomfortable discussing these two topics. Still, we must protect ourselves, our loved ones, and the assets we have accumulated over time. To achieve these goals, you should consider adopting a healthier lifestyle, purchasing life insurance, and making a will.

Best-selling author Robert Fulghum once said in a television interview, "One cannot truly appreciate living until one can understand the process of dying." It sometimes seems as if understanding the finality of death makes us more appreciative of life.

Nevertheless, many of us dislike talking about death or anything associated with it. Hence, many families rarely have a frank discussion about life insurance, wills, or other estate-planning matters—causing needless emotional and economic pain after someone passes away.

It is not only prudent but necessary for households to discuss what to do after a family's breadwinner dies. How will creditors be paid? Will the breadwinner's children be able to attend college? Who will take care of the breadwinner's parents? Who will inherit the deceased's assets? How much money will the deceased's survivors need? If you get your financial house in order while you are alive and well, you can avoid having a probate court step in to answer these questions for you after your death. If you leave these financial matters unattended, you will not have a say in how the probate judge distributes your assets, provides for your family, or puts your financial affairs in order.

Protecting Your Financial Dreams

Many people are under the impression that their financial responsibilities expire when they die, but this is not so. Someone—usually a family member—must get the deceased's financial affairs in order. That task involves paying funeral expenses, paying any unpaid bills, collecting and reviewing important documents, meeting with lawyers and probate judges, disposing of property, and making arrangements for any children or elderly parents. Each year, many families have painfully endured this probate process, which may be understandable if the loved one died suddenly. It is foolish, however, to risk such stress only because you are uncomfortable talking about the financial responsibilities that accompany death. It is a self-imposed gag order that many of us have lived with for too long. Instead, we need to discuss openly how we can protect our dreams—even when faced with death.

Insuring your financial future includes choosing to live a healthy lifestyle, buying life insurance, and preparing a will. When implementing these steps don't focus on estate planning. Instead focus on sharing your good fortune (and insurance) with others. This is what Lavern and her late husband chose to do.

Profile in Courage

Lavern, 48, from Virginia, had worked with her husband to build up a high-tech firm that he ran for 18 years. The couple sold the firm 10 years ago and they retired when Lavern was only 37. After the company was sold, the couple set up a charitable foundation and charitable trusts for their children and grandchildren. When her husband passed away in 1998, the young widow still had financial security, so she devoted her energies to her two passions: philanthropy and her family. She sits on the boards of several charities and is active in fund-raising and development of scholarship funds.

Having financial freedom also allows Lavern to focus time and energy on her nieces and nephews. She travels with them and is involved in their lives in a meaningful way. Lavern is appreciative of "the material things that wealth affords, but the altruistic things are much deeper." She says that being financially secure hasn't really taught her anything new; she always knew that she wanted to help people and give back to her community. "It allowed me to execute. I learned I could be impactful," she says. "Philanthropy is part of who I am right now. I can donate my time and money."

Lavern and her late husband properly planned to protect their income and their financial dreams even if they could not be here to secure them. That is what protecting or insuring your financial dreams is all about.

Your Health May Determine Your Wealth

The significance of choosing a healthier lifestyle becomes clear when you realize that, actuarially speaking, people who are healthy live longer. Having a shorter life span means that less healthy people have less time to earn money, provide for their families, and increase their net worth.

If less healthy American men and women were on an equal playing field with their healthier counterparts, they would add more years of compound interest, more years of earned or Social Security income, and more years of appreciation to their homes and businesses. Adding more years to any investment portfolio represents a significant wealth-building opportunity, and this is especially true for middle-income Americans.

These households must primarily use the time value of money to help their small amount of regular savings grow into larger pools of investment capital. Many factors contribute to the shorter life span of less healthy people—limited access to health care, high-risk diets, poor exercising habits, poverty, discrimination, and an overall lack of awareness about the secrets of longevity. Whatever the causes, the results are the same: Shorter life spans mean a shorter period to increase their household's wealth.

Thus, while less healthy individuals need all the extra time they can get to build their family assets, they are also the households with the least amount of time to do so. What makes matters worse is that sometimes less healthy individuals can take steps to increase their own life span but have chosen not to do so.

The authors of one health guide put it plainly: "In the grand scheme of things, life is a relatively short journey. Sometimes we get so busy trying to earn a living that we forget to take proper care of our health. Proper care of our bodies, however, can improve the quality of our everyday living and give us more time to earn a living and to do those things we enjoy most" (James Reed, Neil Shulman, & Charles Shucker, *The Black Man's Guide to Good Health,* Perigee, 1994).

These authors concluded, "By putting a little effort toward prevention now, we can save ourselves from endless suffering later." For a moment, put aside the economic consequences of death and think about the pain that thousands of households face as they deal with the following realities:

- Heart disease
- Diabetes
- High blood pressure
- Lung cancer
- Smoking
- Obesity
- Breast cancer
- Stroke

Many of these life-threatening illnesses are within our control. Just by choosing a healthier life style, you can dramatically improve your life expectancy. Here are some heartfelt tips:

- Have a regular checkup.
- Restrict the cholesterol in your diet.
- Stop smoking.
- Exercise regularly.
- Lose weight.
- Take your medication.
- Encourage your friends and family to join you in your new lifestyle.
- Share healthy cooking tips with your friends.
- Suggest that your religious and community groups hold blood pressure screenings.
- Find partners to exercise with several times a week.
- Ask your employer to offer healthful choices in the company vending machines and cafeteria.
- Start a fitness walking club or exercise class at work.
- Urge your favorite food market and restaurants to offer a wide selection of healthful foods.

These suggestions point also to the importance of more American households taking a stand for good health. Viewing good health as an economic tool may help many households take this important stand. Health and wealth are inexorably linked. It is hard to deny that your health will often indicate how wealthy you are or will become. Therefore, those of us who dare to play the financial success game must also choose to adopt a healthier lifestyle.

Moderation in all things is not just a slogan, but a way to achieve the financial success we desire. What good is it to achieve financial success if you will not be around to enjoy it? A verse in the Bible states, "When I was a child, I spoke like a child, I thought like a child. . . . But when I became an adult, I put my childish ways aside" (1 Corinthians 13:11). For our discussion of winning the wealth-building game, we may paraphrase this verse to say, "When I was less healthy, I acted like I was less healthy. But when I decided to become healthier, I put my less healthy and lifeshortening ways aside."

Insuring Your Future Income

Like many financial products, life insurance can be confusing. And sometimes, overly trained insurance agents can make selecting the right insurance program even more confusing. Insurance salespeople can be creative when talking about the benefits of their products. I found this out recently when I wanted to learn more about universal life insurance.

To better understand this product, I invited three insurance people to come to my office to explain to me how their insurance could meet my needs. The first insurance agent explained to me, "Universal life insurance is the best insurance product that was ever created." As he explained it, "this one insurance product could cover me from the basket to the casket." After he made his presentation, he gave me some literature to read, and if I do say so, I was very impressed.

That was until the second insurance agent arrived. He told me that he had a better universal life insurance product. I asked, "You have something better than the basket to the casket?" He explained, "My company's universal life plan can cover you from the womb to the tomb." Now I was really impressed. He, too, gave me some literature to read after his presentation.

By the time the third agent arrived, I had made up my mind. I was going to go with the womb-to-the-tomb universal life plan. When I shared this with the third insurance agent, he told me he had a better product. I gasped, "You have something better than the womb to the tomb?" The agent replied, "Sir, my company's universal life plan can cover you from conception to resurrection."

What is interesting is that all three were selling the same product. Had I not taken time to do my own research, I could have been overwhelmed by a sales pitch and purchased an insurance product that might not have been suitable for my situation.

Most people know that the term *life insurance* is a misnomer in the sense that it cannot replace a person's life. What life insurance can do is replace a substantial part of the insured's income. Hence, it becomes protection to replace future earnings that may be lost due to a person's untimely death.

According to the American Council of Life Insurance, a trade group in Washington, DC, the average American family has $200,000 in insurance coverage. Every year consumers take billions of dollars in insurance coverage. Despite all that protection, the National Insurance Consumers Organization in Alexandria, Virginia, reports, "Twenty percent (20 percent) of all policies are dropped after two years, and almost 50 percent (50 percent) of all policies are cashed out after ten years" (2004 study).

Additionally, the American Council of Life Insurance reported that the average size policy for each insured person was $75,000 and that most insurance policies were purchased by men to protect the income needs of their families. The average married couple owns $150,000 of life insurance coverage.

While some American families view life insurance as income protection, too many households are underinsured because they still view life insurance simply as a way to pay for funeral or burial expenses. This may account for the small amount of life insurance Americans own, and the reason we view life insurance as a death-related financial product as opposed to a life-enriching tool that can help the deceaseds' loved ones. Sometimes while trying to ensure that family members are buried with dignity, we fail to make sure that the deceaseds' income can be replaced, so that their survivors can live with dignity.

Most families have two estates—their current estate and their future estate. Their current estate is represented by the tangible property they currently own, whereas their future estate is represented by the assets they will acquire with their future earnings. All American households should have life insurance protection to protect their future estates. When I discuss insuring your financial dreams, I am referring to using insurance to protect your unacquired future earnings.

Many families believe that they cannot afford more than a few thousand dollars of life insurance. Likewise, instead of term insurance, many families are persuaded to buy whole-life insurance or universal-whole-life insurance. Both types represent high-cost insurance plans that could provide very little actual protection. Another name for these policies is *cash value life insurance*. The name refers to the so-called savings or cash value accumulation within the life insurance policy. In essence, these policies combine a savings plan with a term insurance policy.

There have been several excellent books written about the fallacies, abuses, and problems associated with cash value insurance polices. The most widely respected one is *What's Wrong with Your Life Insurance?* by Norman F. Dacey (Macmillan, 1989). For several reasons, cash value life insurance plans may not be the best choice to reach your financial goals. There are times when a universal life whole life policy may be your best choice to save money, defer taxes, or protect your estate from estate tax erosion. In most situations, however, purchasing an *annual-decreasing-term-to-age-65* or a *level-*

term-to-age-65 life insurance policy is all a family needs. This type of insurance policy:

- Provides the maximum protection.
- Is often less expensive.
- Is a simple, understandable life insurance program.

All life insurance premiums are based on mortality tables. Historical data helps insurance companies predict the average life span of any given group of people of a certain age, income, and state of health. On the basis of this information, life insurance companies can establish their mortality rates or cost per $1,000 of insurance for a particular age group.

When you buy term insurance, you are paying for just your natural mortality rate. When you buy a cash value policy, you pay for your natural mortality rate, plus money that is placed in a saving or investment side fund within the policy. Because term insurance lets you pay for your natural mortality rate, many financial planning professionals refer to term insurance as buying "pure protection."

When you buy term insurance, every year, your cost will match your increased mortality rate. Additionally, at age 65, you will find yourself with only a small amount of life insurance protection or no insurance protection at all. This will not be an issue for you if you have taken the advice in this book and invested a small portion of your earnings every month. At age 65, you should be self-insured, meaning you have enough liquid assets to pay for your funeral with enough left over to leave to your heirs.

Another reason I suggest term insurance is its affordability. In addition to needing money to bury their loved ones, many people need money to provide for their children, and to pay for the family car or home. When you add all these expenditures, it is easy to see how a $10,000 or $50,000 whole-life insurance plan won't be enough.

In fact, most financial planning professionals suggest that a family's insurance policy be at least five times the breadwinners' income. A household where both spouses earn $100,000 would need $500,000 in insurance protection on both spouses. The payments on $500,000 of whole-life or any cash value insurance is expensive, compared with $500,000 of term insurance, which is affordable for most households. It is not uncommon for cash value life insurance to cost 10 times more than term insurance for the same protection.

A third reason for buying term insurance is that it is an easy-to-understand policy. Don't invest in anything that you don't understand and can't explain to a friend in five minutes. This advice is relevant whether you are talking about a business venture, a new mutual fund, or life insurance.

Many fast-talking insurance salespeople will try to convince you that you can understand all the bells and whistles associated with a cash value insurance plan. In reality, cash value insurance plans are so convoluted that even many insurance professionals don't understand the product they are selling. Insurance representatives often make the biggest commissions on cash value policies and the least commission on term insurance policies. Which would you sell? There is an old saying in the insurance business, "If you sell term insurance, you can't eat, but when you sell whole life insurance, you can't sleep." Guess why?

In any case, you don't need bells or whistles when you buy insurance; you just need income protection. You need to protect your financial dreams, which are in jeopardy if you die prematurely. Term insurance can provide you the basic income protection you need—it is simple to understand, and it usually offers maximum protection at a reasonable price.

Your Money and Your Life

By using term insurance, you can provide your family with needed insurance protection as well as have additional money to save for your long-term investment goals. By investing your extra money instead of letting an insurance company invest for you in a whole-life policy, you will get a better return. Also, you will have complete control and access to these funds whenever you need them.

A word of advice: If you do not have the intestinal fortitude to buy term insurance and invest the money on your own, then you may be better served buying a universal-life insurance policy. These policies will at least let you invest a portion of your savings in mutual funds. Universal-life policies are very expensive, and have many hidden costs. Nevertheless, if you can't buy term and invest the rest on your own, then this may be your best alternative.

Protecting Your Current Income

In addition to term insurance, there are several other pure insurance products that can help you insure your financial dreams. Disability insurance can pay up to 60 percent of your income if you are sick, disabled, and unable to work.

Depending on the type of policy you purchased, you could be assured an income for your lifetime or until age 65 if you are permanently disabled. Most disability policies are pure protection policies and therefore don't have a cash fund that will increase your premium payments.

Millionaire in the Making

When Joyce walks into a room her positive presence lights up the entire space. Her aura is so bright that one barely notices the handsome cane she uses to support her measured steps. Her warm smile and southern charm completely conceal the many years of physical pain and emotional anguish she has had to endure.

Joyce is a successful lawyer, jewelry designer, and political fundraiser. She has traveled extensively and met with some of the world's most powerful and influential people. Her Maryland-based high-end jewelry design firm employed more than 100 people. But all of this came to an abrupt halt when a truck hit Joyce's car while she was driving on the New Jersey Turnpike.

The accident left Joyce with a broken neck and severe injuries to many parts of her body. Five years, ten operations, and countless therapy sessions later, Joyce is thankful to be alive. She is still trying to secure restitution from the driver who hit her car and his insurance provider. Confidently, Joyce takes it all in stride, as she tries to restore the full use of her body along with her professional and personal life.

Joyce's soft-spoken manner camouflages the depth of her wisdom and inner strength. During those emotionally and physically draining years she had to close her beloved jewelry business. While focusing on her recovery she also had to make a number of major financial decisions. Because, in spite of her dire physical condition she still had to eat, sleep, pay her bills, and most important, pay her healthcare providers. Sadly, she had to do all of this by herself, with little emotional or financial support from others. "I am glad I had my own disability insurance," Joyce said. "That's what (financially) saved me." Today, Joyce is heroically taking steps to rebuild her jewelry design business. She is a profile in courage and her story of per-

sonal bravery illustrates why all of us should own a personal disability in-surance policy.

Not as apparent, but just as beneficial to insuring a family's future estate are company-sponsored insurance plans, family insurance riders, waivers of premiums, disability insurance riders, and mortgage insurance.

Notice, I did not add "consumer credit insurance policies." These policies are basically products that increase salespeople's commission by selling you a life insurance policy to pay off a small consumer loan, should you die. A large term insurance policy will often enable your family to pay off these consumer loans; therefore, you do not need to purchase credit insurance policies. Here are a few other ideas for you to keep in mind when insuring your financial dreams.

Go with the Best: Always Choose a Triple-A Rated Insurance Company

Free ratings on any insurance company can be requested from Standard & Poor's or Moody's. Both are listed in the Resource Guide.

Ask for Referrals

Get three referrals from people you trust when looking for a reputable in-surance agent. Interview all three, evaluating them on the following points:

- Does the agent listen to you?
- Does the agent answer your questions and explain things to you, or do you get a sales pitch?
- When you call, do you receive a prompt response?
- Before making recommendations, does the agent review your finan-cial situation?
- Do you receive an itemized breakdown of all the fees, charges, and commissions?
- Does the agent show you realistic illustrations or examples?

All Insurance Companies Want to Make a Profit

Avoid being persuaded that a mutual insurance company is better than a stock company. Both sell life insurance for a profit, and the so-called dividends that mutual companies share with their policyholders are not investment dividends, but a creation that insurance companies refer to as *insurance dividends*. In reality, insurance dividends are nothing more than a return of your excess premium payment. So, if you really want to share in the profits of an insurance company, you must do what other investors do, and buy the insurance company's stock.

Get a Safe-Deposit Box

Place your insurance papers and will in a safe, centrally located place and make sure your family knows its location in case of an emergency.

Let Your Will Be Known

Because we often avoid discussing death-related financial matters, many households do not have a written will. Wills are a necessary part of insuring your financial dreams; they are important for no other reason than to let people know how to distribute your insurance proceeds. Furthermore, a will lets people know how you want your future estate to be distributed, managed, and protected. When people leave an estate without a will, the court and state make all these decisions without the benefit of the deceased's insight.

Everyone needs a will regardless of the size of the estate. A will is a legal document that tells your family members how to divide and share your money and possessions. Wills specify who is to inherit what. Wills are fairly easy and inexpensive to prepare, and you can find a do-it-yourself guide at any bookstore or legal form web site.

Moneywise Master Class

Charles Gonzales is the author of *Si Se Puede: Every Latino's Guide To Building Family Wealth*. He is also a regular on the *Moneywise* program. There I asked him to share his thoughts about insurance. Here is what he had to say:

BOSTON: Charles, how can insurance protect someone's assets?
GONZALES: Life insurance and disability insurance products essentially take the risk of losing your asset, from your own shoulders and plac-

ing it on the shoulders of an insurance company. In return for that safety or getting rid of the risk of losing everything, you pay a small premium to the insurance company.

BOSTON: It is a product many people don't like to discuss.

GONZALES: People don't like to talk about insurance, period. It is something that is negative, that they have bad feelings about.

BOSTON: But what are you telling people to help them overcome their apprehension about purchasing insurance?

GONZALES: People buy life insurance for the most part because there's love in the equation somewhere. But the main reason my clients are interested in purchasing life insurance is because they care about someone.

BOSTON: What about disability insurance?

GONZALES: Everybody needs disability insurance to protect their income. People under the age of 40 have a greater chance of becoming disabled than they do of dying, and it's unfortunate that people overlook disability planning.

BOSTON: Is disability insurance expensive, and can an individual buy it on their own?

GONZALES: Disability insurance can be customized to fit your particular needs. You can get a disability policy that will cover you just for two years, five years, ten years.

BOSTON: What is the most important thing people should know about insurance?

GONZALES: The role that life and disability insurance products play in an overall game plan or financial strategy. Asset protection represents the foundation of your financial plan.

When insuring your income, remember to choose a healthier lifestyle, purchase the proper life insurance protection, and make a will. Also remember not to focus on estate planning, but on sharing your good fortune (and insurance) with others. If you remember these tips when insuring your income, you can protect your financial dreams and reduce your fear of discussing mortality. Now review the information covered in this chapter.

MASTER KEYS

Know

By their fruits ye shall know them.

—*Matthew 7:20*

Act

Think less about mortality and more about insuring your dreams.

Adopt a healthier lifestyle.

Review your insurance plan.

Make a will.

Compare term and whole life insurance costs.

Make sure you have a triple-A rated company.

Purchase your own disability insurance plan.

Believe

It is a joy to plan and share my good fortune
(or insurance) with others!

9

STARTING A BUSINESS ENTERPRISE

> We are all in the gutter, but some of us are looking at the stars.
>
> —*Oscar Wilde*

EMOTIONAL FACTOR:
Fear of Failure

Many people are terrified of being self-employed because they are afraid that they will lose all their savings, assets, and good reputation if their business is unsuccessful. They may also fear that they will lose control of their personal life, as if this doesn't happen in corporate America.

Such apprehensions may explain why, relatively speaking, only a few brave souls choose self-employment as their profession. Naturally, people who are afraid of being self-employed rarely consider owning a business. This is unfortunate because they are overlooking one of the best ways to acquire wealth in the United States.

Small business owners have more control over their financial destiny than you might think. This chapter explains how to start a small business enterprise and describes the traits many successful business owners share.

You may find this information useful even if you never own a business: (1) It will diminish your fears of business ownership; (2) it will reduce the likelihood that you will transfer your small business phobia to others (many of whom may work in a small business enterprise). Such transference could aversely impact a person's livelihood and the bottom line of the small business where that employee works.

Because many Americans work in small business operations, it is important to understand how small business enterprises can help you become financially successful. Starting small helped Guillermo cope with his fear of being self employed.

Profile in Courage

Guillermo was a teenager when he came to the United States from his native Panama in the 1970s. He had learned English in school, but his real education came when he got here, he says, and he learned as he went along.

After high school graduation, Guillermo found work as a plumber's assistant. His job was to dig the ditches for the plumber to lay the pipes. Eventually, he started helping and as the company saw that he was capable, they trained him. He became a master plumber, and over time, he obtained other licenses as well: journeyman, master mechanic (HVAC), then gas fitter.

He still wanted more. He realized that he could put all these trades together and become a home inspector. He had some savings, and so he decided to start his own business. This was no simple matter. Guillermo knew it would be an uphill climb because, at that time (in the mid-1980s), it was difficult for minorities to break into the home inspection business. He knew that he would have to work twice as hard and be twice as good as anyone else. In addition, he had a wife and child to think about.

Guillermo was scared, but he had a vision. So he did his research, figured out what steps he needed to take and how much everything was going to cost.

He sat down with his wife and went through his plan. "I have a supportive wife," he says, "we talked about it and made some adjustments. We cut our spending."

Guillermo admits that he couldn't have done it if his wife wasn't support-ive. She had to continue working full time as a registered nurse to provide fi-nancial support. She also provided emotional support and stood by him through the difficult early days. "She realized it was a vision and a goal," he says. "She heard my heart beat that I wanted to do this."

Despite her support and his research, Guillermo still had to overcome his fear of jumping into the unknown. So he started small. He designed a logo. That's it. A simple thing. But once he had taken that first step, it was easier to take the second, and then continue through. Three years later, Guillermo's wife was able to quit working full time.

"She has seen the vision come to fruition," he says of his wife. And now, eight years later, Guillermo has a successful business and helps others start their own businesses. He has what he calls a three-step process—vision, plan, execution: "Take the vision out of your heart and put it on paper. Figure out what you need to do, and how much everything will cost. Then it becomes a plan. Finally, execute that plan." He counsels those who are afraid to take the final step of executing the plan to do what he did. "I encourage them to look through their plan and find one thing to start with. Get a license, get a name, file the papers."

Guillermo has also learned that since he faced his fear, he now can man-age it. He currently fears that his business will grow too fast and that he will have more customers than he can handle. "I like to do things systematically and to keep in control," he says. But his fears don't get the best of him. Guillermo is a good example of an entrepreneur.

What Is an Entrepreneur?

Because the word *entrepreneur* evokes so many images, I thought that it would be good to define how I use the term. Jeffry A. Timmons offers us a complete definition of entrepreneurship in his insightful book, *The Entre-preneurial Mind* (Brick House Publishing, 1989). There, he writes:

Entrepreneurship is the ability to create and build something from practically nothing. It is initiating, doing, achieving, and building an enterprise or organization, rather than just watching, analyzing or describing one. It is the knack for sensing an opportunity where others see chaos, contradiction and confusion. It is the ability to build a founding team to complement your own skills and talents. It is the know-how to find, marshal and control resources (often owned by others) and to make sure you don't run out of money when you need it most. Finally, it is a willingness to take calculated risks, both personal and financial, and then do everything possible to get the odds in your favor. (p. 1)

Timmons also noted, "While anyone can try to start a business, relatively few can grow one to beyond $1 million in sales. According to government data, only about 1 in 30 businesses have annual sales of over $1 million."

In this work, Timmons also suggests the size a business needs to be for success. The businesses with the most likelihood of experiencing long-term success have a minimum of 10 employees and sales over $500,000. His research also points out, "Survival odds, and prosperity—namely, significant job creation—improve even further once the $1 million in sales level is attained."

Twelve Myths about Entrepreneurship

Folklore and stereotypes about entrepreneurs are remarkably durable, even in these informed and sophisticated times. Here are 12 myths and realities of entrepreneurship that Timmons has compiled:

Myth 1: Entrepreneurs are born, not made.

Reality: There is increasing evidence that successful entrepreneurs emerge from a combination of work experience, study, and development of appropriate skills. While there are, no doubt, attributes that you either have or you don't, possessing them does not necessarily an entrepreneur make, and other skills of equal importance can, in fact, be acquired through understanding, hard work, and patience.

Myth 2: Anyone can start a business. It's a matter of luck and guts. All you need is a new idea; then go for it.

Reality: If you want to launch and grow a high-potential venture, you must get the odds in your favor. You cannot think and act like an inventor, or a promoter, or even a manager; you must think and act like an entrepreneur.

Myth 3: Entrepreneurs are gamblers. They roll the dice and take the consequences.

Reality: Successful entrepreneurs are very careful to calculate the risks they take. They get others to share risk with them, thereby lowering their personal exposure. When they find they can avoid or minimize risks, they do so.

Myth 4: You are better off as an independent, sole entrepreneur, owning the whole show yourself.

Reality: It is extremely difficult to grow a venture beyond $1 million in profitable sales working single-handedly. Ventures that succeed usually have multiple founders. Besides, 100 percent of nothing is nothing.

Myth 5: Being an entrepreneur is the only way you can really be your own boss and completely independent.

Reality: Entrepreneurs are far from independent, and have many masters and constituencies to serve and juggle: partners, investors, customers, suppliers, creditors, employees, spouse, family, social, and community obligations.

Myth 6: Entrepreneurs work longer and harder than managers in big companies.

Reality: The self-employed actually work no more or less time than their corporate counterparts.

Myth 7: Entrepreneurs face greater stress and more pressures, and thus pay a higher price for their role than any others.

Reality: Being an entrepreneur is stressful and demanding. But there is no evidence that it is any more stressful than other demanding professional roles, such as a partner in a large accounting or law firm, or head of a large corporation or government agency. Most entrepreneurs enjoy what they do; they reported more fun than drudgery; they thrived on the flexibility and innovative aspects of their jobs. Studies show that entrepreneurs report very high job satisfaction.

Myth 8: Starting your own company is a risky, hazardous proposition which often ends in failure.

Reality: Success, rather than failure, is more common among higher potential ventures because they are driven by talented and experienced founders in pursuit of attractive opportunities, who are able to attract both the right people and necessary financial and other resources to make the venture work.

Myth 9: Money makes the difference. If you have enough working capital, you will succeed.

Reality: Money is the least important ingredient in a new venture's success. If the other pieces and talents are there, the money will follow. Money is not a prime motivator, either. Entrepreneurs thrive on the "thrill of the chase." Time and again, even after they have made a few million dollars, they still work long hours and launch more companies.

Myth 10: Start-ups are for the young and energetic.

Reality: While these qualities may help, it appears that age is no barrier to a start-up, and can have advantages, such as well-developed networks of contacts. Numerous examples exist of start-ups whose founders were over 60.

Myth 11: Entrepreneurs are motivated solely by the quest for the almighty dollar; they want to make money so they can spend it.

Reality: Growth-minded entrepreneurs are more driven by building the enterprise and realizing long-term capital gains than by instant gratification through high salaries and perks. A sense of personal achievement and accomplishment, feeling in control of their own destinies, and realizing their vision and dreams are also powerful motivators. Money is viewed as a tool and a way of keeping score.

Myth 12: Entrepreneurs seek power and control over others so they can feel in charge.

Reality: While many entrepreneurs are driven this way, most successful growth-minded entrepreneurs are just the opposite. They are driven by the quest for responsibility, achievement, and results, rather than power. They thrive on a sense of accomplishment from outperforming the competition, rather than by a personal need for power expressed by dominating and controlling others. They gain control by their results.

Starting a Business

More than likely, your first business venture would be under $1 million in annual sales. Such companies are categorized by the U.S. government as small businesses. Nevertheless, do not let this nomenclature fool you, because small businesses mean big business for the owner and for the country.

According to the U.S. Department of Labor small businesses create most of the new jobs in this country. Additionally, small businesses create huge income and net worth potential for their owners. Each year, thousands of business owners increase their net worth substantially by starting a small business.

The Right Time to Start

When is the right time to begin your own business? Many potential business owners ponder this question and often get caught up in it far too long, as the time never seems to be right. They say they'll take the plunge when they save more money, when the children graduate from school, after the mortgage is paid off, or when they retire. Although each of these is a good reason not to quit your job just to start your own business, they are not reasons to postpone starting the process. Starting any venture requires planning, saving, and researching. Waiting to begin this process could be detrimental to your success. If the feeling is right, then the time is right. As they say at Nike, "Just do it."

If you know that owning a business is what you want, then begin your planning today. Set your timetable and start the process. If you do it properly, it could be the most rewarding experience of your life. This is what happened to Monique.

Millionaire in the Making

Monique and her husband recently opened their third bed-and-breakfast in her hometown of Washington, DC. In 1995, while editor in chief for a national magazine, Monique converted an old mansion in Brooklyn, New York, into her first B&B.

According to Monique, "I just stepped out on faith and built this bed-and-breakfast, and was quite surprised when the majority of my guests came from down the street and around the corner." When she opened her first inn, Monique continued to work part-time. But in less than a year, she was working full-time managing her business. Monique says, "I enjoyed staying at bed-and-breakfast inns as a guest, and the more I stayed at inns, I realized that innkeeping combined all of my personal passions. I love to decorate, I love to entertain, I fall in love with buildings. Just about everything except for the cooking part, and I learned to love that as well."

The couple used their own money to finance their first bed-and-breakfast. Later, they used their equity to open other B&Bs in Cape May, New Jersey, and now, Washington, DC. By buying distressed properties, Monique could purchase them below market price and turn them into unique inns. She believes many women are afraid to start their own businesses.

According to Monique, "I think the thing that paralyzes women especially when it comes to starting their own business is fear. But at the same time I think that if you prepare yourself and you know you're ready, you've done the research, maybe you did an apprenticeship, you've crossed all your t's and dotted all your i's, if you have a fallback plan. Then Go for It."

While a success now, the company has been through difficult times. But according to Monique, it has been worth it. "There's nothing like creating your own vision and making it happen, bringing it to fruition. I work harder than I ever worked for anybody else, but it's on my own terms."

Success and Failure

Let's not make light of the fact that proper planning is extremely important. The statistics on the failure rate of small businesses in this country are staggering. In 2004, the U.S. Department of Commerce reports that 80 percent of new businesses closed by year-end from 2000 to 2003.

With this information at hand, I contend that the primary difference between the successes and the failures is proper preparation. A very large percentage of new businesses fail within the first two years. The problems that occur in the early stages of business operation should have been addressed in the planning stage. Here are the causes of most of these failures:

- Lack of research.
- Improper marketing.
- Improper management.
- Lack of capital.
- Lack of technology.

Early-stage planning should include each of these areas, and some of the tasks, especially writing the business plan, should be done with the help of professionals. Every potential business owner must address capitalizing the enterprise in the early planning stage, although this may not be the only time that capitalization becomes an issue. There are many causes of small business failure, but lack of capital is easy to detect and remains the number one reason for most of the failed enterprises.

Owners often blame their company's problems on lack of capital when, in fact, a multitude of other problems are causing the capital problem. Although sometimes lack of capital is legitimately a company's only problem, it usually signifies inadequate planning.

Using Savings for Start-Up Capital

There are various sources of start-up funding that a new business owner can tap. Savings are the most popular way to fund business ventures. Many business owners use this source because they don't know of any other way to obtain cash. Savings can also be the least expensive source of capital, free from fees and interest. If you have enough money saved to finance your endeavor, and you decide to use savings as your source of capitalization, make sure you have a backup plan. Often the start-up process may stall because of mistakes or unforeseen situations that make it necessary to secure additional capital.

Loans

The most traditional source for borrowing is your local bank. Banks are typically conservative in their small business lending departments, and many will not even consider start-ups with less than three years of operation. But, if the business has passed that threshold, banks are worth checking out. They may also consider small start-up loans if you can offer substantial collateral, such as your house.

Applying for a small business loan is generally an in-depth process. Because of the failure rate of small businesses, the banker will typically want as much collateral as possible, as well as a personal guarantee to complete the deal. A personal guarantee is a promissory note to repay the loan should the business venture fail. The banker will also perform a thorough analysis of your plans with a trained, constructive, and critical eye. Make sure that the information you submit is correct and complete because first impressions are extremely important. The bank will assess three primary factors in your application: *credit, collateral,* and *character.* These will be the basis for their decision to approve or deny your loan request.

An *asset-based* loan is another borrowing vehicle that may be available to you. Asset-based loans are generally used with companies that have been in business for some specific period. This loan is secured by a specific operational asset of the business, typically accounts receivable or machinery and equipment.

There are also many *investment-based* lending institutions that pool together funds from investors to make nontraditional high-risk loans to businesses. These organizations can be difficult to locate because they are usually classified as investment organizations rather than as lending organizations. This kind of loan is generally expensive and should not be the first choice for capitalizing your business endeavor. It should only be entertained as a last resort.

Many local governments participate in loan programs tailored to small businesses. Local and state governments have programs that stress locating in certain areas and creating jobs. The federal government and the Small Business Administration have several loan programs available. You can ask your banker about these loans. Usually government loans have lower interest rates than any of the other borrowing vehicles we have discussed because the government wants to promote the continued creation of small business in this country.

Equity Partners

Another way to capitalize your business endeavor is to sell stock in your company. You must first, however, formulate your idea and plan, and present them to your prospective stock buyers. At this level of business, you should only give this information to people you know in some way. You must be careful about sharing your ideas with others. You wouldn't be the first person to have an idea that someone else cashes in on. There are two types of stock that you can sell: common and preferred. Common stock is a way that others can buy into your business, and you can raise capital that does not have to be paid back. However, with this sale, you lose some control of your business. Common stock represents ownership; therefore, it is important not to sell too much common stock, or you could lose control of your business. Just remember to retain at least 51 percent of the common stock available at all times. On the other hand, you could sell preferred stock, which is nonvoting stock. This means that the stock purchaser has no ownership in the business. You can sell as much preferred stock as possible without any control issues. However, the preferred stockholder must be paid back, usually at a premium, sometime in the future. This type of stock is sometimes referred to as *quasi-equity,* because it starts off as equity and after a period of time (1 year, 5 years, or 10 years), it converts to debt.

Venture Capital

Venture capital is another source for raising capital. Venture capitalists are groups of investors who have pooled funds to invest in selected companies or ideas for companies. These investors generally look for companies with ideas that are on the forefront of technology in any particular industry. The cost of this type of funding is typically paid to the venture capital group in the form of common or preferred stock, depending on the situation.

Securing small business capital to start and grow your business can be daunting. When you are going through this process, it may seem like it is taking forever. Just remember that your loan processors must do their *due diligence.* The due diligence process is a thorough background check lenders perform on business owners prior to lending them funds. Their thorough investigation is not a personal reflection on you or your business enterprise. Companies that provide capital have to protect their depositors and investors' money by not capitalizing money-losing business ventures.

You may have heard the story about the time a banker called in an oil-man to review his loans. "We loaned you a million dollars to revive your old wells, and they went dry" said the banker. "Could have been worse," the oilman replied. "Then we loaned you a million to drill new wells, and they were dry," the banker continued. "Could have been worse," the oilman replied. "Then we loaned you another million for new drilling equipment, and it broke down," said the banker. "Could have been worse," replied the oilman. "I'm getting tired of hearing that!" snapped the banker. "How could it have been worse?" he asked. "Could have been my money," replied the oilman.

Be patient and do what you can to ease your financial supporter's worry about ever needing to have this kind of discussion with you. Having a well-written business plan will help you secure your loan and reduce your financial backer's concerns.

Writing Your Business Plan

Your business plan should cover the following information: a description of your business and its products or services, your location, who your customers will be, where you can find them, what you will charge for the business's products and services, what kind of advertising you will use, how much it will cost, who your competition is, your business strengths and weaknesses, who will manage your operation, what management skills and background they have, how much it will cost to start this business, what your personal investment will be, where additional capital will come from (if applicable), what your projected earnings and expenses are, and what your projected net income will be. The business plan should be a comprehensive presentation of your expected business venture. Because of its importance, you will need professional help in putting it together, or you will at least need to find a good business guide with a sample plan in your bookstore or computer software store. The Small Business Administration and SCORE (Service Corps of Retired Executives) both provide excellent help to small business owners in writing business plans. Their contact information can be found in the Resource Guide.

The Pros and Cons of Entrepreneurship

Before you rush out the door to start your enterprise, let's review the advantages and disadvantages of owning a business. Too often, business failure can be directly attributed to entrepreneurs who go into business for the wrong reason. In fact, if you are considering going into business for any reason other than creating a financially successful organization, then you are going into business for the wrong reason. The following lists of advantages and disadvantages can help you decide whether entrepreneurship is the right choice for you:

Advantages

- You are your own boss and don't have to report to some superior.
- For better or worse, you have the independence and power to make your own business decisions. Many entrepreneurs find that this is one of the major payoffs of having their own businesses.
- There is direct contact with customers, employees, suppliers, and others.
- Personal satisfaction and a sense of achievement come with being a success, plus the recognition that goes with it. For most successful entrepreneurs, money is not the real goal, but merely a way of keeping score in the game of business.
- You can be creative and develop your own idea, product, or service; you have the chance to make a living doing something you truly enjoy.
- You are doing something that contributes to others, whether it be providing an excellent product or service, providing employment, paying dividends to stockholders, or doing something else that is useful or creates value.

If you are like most people, you may not have thought much about the downside. Awareness of the potential disadvantages of going into business for yourself should not discourage you if you have a strong commitment to that goal. However, forewarned is forearmed, It will not be helpful for you to have an unrealistic view of the business world.

Disadvantages

- In many ways, you are still not your own boss. Instead of having one boss, you will now have many—your customers, the government agencies to which you must report, and, in some cases, your key suppliers.
- There is a large financial risk. The failure rate is high in new businesses, and you may lose not only your own money, but also that of the friends and relatives who may have bankrolled you.

- The hours are long and hard. When you start your business, you will no longer be working 9 to 5. Count on working 10, 12, or even 15-hour days, often 6 or 7 days a week.
- You will not have much spare time for family or a social life. And you can forget about taking any long vacations for the next few years, since the business is unlikely to run itself without your presence for any great length of time.
- Unlike a salary, your income will not be steady. You may make more or less than you could working for someone else, but in either case, your income could fluctuate from month to month.
- The buck stops with you. If a problem arises, there is no boss to whom you can say, "What do we do about this?" You are the boss now, and all the responsibility is yours. If anything goes wrong, the cost comes out of your pocket.
- You may be stuck for years doing work you do not like. Unlike an employee, you cannot simply quit and look for a better job. If you decide you don't like what you are doing, it may take years for you to sell the business or find some other way to get out of it without a major financial loss.

Now, if you still feel that you have what it takes to be an entrepreneur—Congratulations! You have reviewed the requirements more carefully than many people who have made the leap into business ownership. To confirm your belief in your potential to own a small business, complete Form 9.1 (Checklist for Going into Business).

Buying an Existing Business

Buying an existing business can have a positive effect on your net worth. To buy an existing business, you must first identify a business with undervalued assets. The assets may not be fully valued because of the economic climate, the inability of management to produce to the assets' capacity, the bad name that the business created because of unfair or poor business practice, or a number of other reasons. Once you have identified the business, whether it is for sale or not, you must next assess whether you can turn the

Form 9.1
Checklist for Going into Business

Under each question, check the answer that says what you feel or comes closest to it. Be honest with yourself.

Are you a self-starter?
_____ I do things on my own. Nobody has to tell me to get going.
_____ If someone gets me started, I keep going all night.
_____ Easy does it. I don't put myself out until I have to.

How do you feel about other people?
_____ I like people. I can get along with just about anybody.
_____ I have plenty of friends—I don't need anybody else.
_____ Most people irritate me.

Can you lead others?
_____ I can get most people to go along when I start something.
_____ I can give orders if someone tells me what we should do.
_____ I let someone else get things moving. Then I go along if I feel like it.

Can you take responsibility?
_____ I like to take charge of things and see them through.
_____ I'll take over if I have to, but I'd rather let someone else be responsible.
_____ There's always some eager beaver around wanting to show how smart he is. I say, let him.

How good an organizer are you?
_____ I like to have a plan before I start. I'm usually the one to get things lined up when the group wants to do something.
_____ I do all right unless things get too confused. Then I quit.
_____ You get all set and then something comes along and presents too many problems. So I just take things as they come.

How good a worker are you?
_____ I can keep going as long as I need to. I don't mind working hard for something I want.
_____ I'll work hard for a while, but when I've had enough, that's it.
_____ I can't see that hard work gets you anywhere.

Can you make decisions?
_____ I can make up my mind in a hurry if I have to. It usually turns out okay, too.
_____ I can if I have plenty of time. If I have to make up my mind fast, I think later I should have decided the other way.
_____ I don't like to be the one who has to decide things.

(continued)

Form 9.1 *(Continued)*

Can people trust what you say?

_____ You bet they can. I don't say things I don't mean.

_____ I try to be on the level most of the time, but sometimes I just say what's easiest.

_____ Why bother if the other fellow doesn't know the difference?

Can you stick with it?

_____ If I make up my mind to do something, I don't let anything stop me.

_____ I usually finish what I start—if it goes well.

_____ If it doesn't go right away, I quit. Why beat your brains out?

How good is your health?

_____ I never run down!

_____ I have enough energy for most things I want to do.

_____ I run out of energy sooner than most of my friends seem to.

Now count the checks you made.

How many checks are there beside the first answer to each question?_____

How many checks are there beside the second answer to each question?_____

How many checks are there beside the third answer to each question?_____

If most of your checks are beside the first question, you probably have what it takes to run a business. If not, you're likely to have more trouble than you can handle by yourself. Better find a partner who is strong on the points you're weak on. If many checks are beside the third answer, not even a good partner will be able to shore you up.

Source: Jeffry A. Timmons, *The Entrepreneurial Mind* (Brickhouse Publishing, 1989), "Checklist for Going into Business," Small Marketers Aids #71.

operation around so that the assets can experience full value under your management.

Unless you are part of the staff or the business that is for sale, this may be difficult. If your assessment is positive—meaning you can increase the value of the assets of the business—make an offer. The offer should be equal to the market value of the assets, in addition to any intangible worth the business may have. The diligence to assess the potential should be done by professionals—a certified public accountant and an attorney. If you are successful in turning the business in the right direction, and as a result increase the value of the company, your net worth will increase as well.

Moneywise Master Class

One of the biggest challenges of starting a business is finding the money to fund it. To share her insight on how to secure business capital, Faye Coleman, president of Westover Consultants Incorporated, a management consulting firm appeared on the *Moneywise* program. Here is a portion of our discussion:

BOSTON: How hard is it to find financing to start a business?

COLEMAN: It depends on your particular situation and the amount of money you're looking for. One of the keys for would-be entrepreneurs is to make sure that they've taken stock of their own personal financial situation. They need to be aware of their own assets, their own liability, so that we know what they are bringing to the table and then we can identify the amounts needed based on a good business plan and then identify the correct lender.

BOSTON: How do you find the bank that's right for you?

COLEMAN: They need to look at a couple of key things. The amount of the loan they're looking for? What are the uses of those funds once they receive them? The bank is not just interested in you saying just in general, I need $100,000 for operating capital. Most people throw that around all the time and it's not true working capital that they need. What they need is equipment. They may need to make some leasehold improvements.

BOSTON: How important is a business plan?

COLEMAN: A business plan is key, especially if you're a start-up. No bank wants to look at you, sit down and talk with you if you don't have a business plan. There are quite a few places that you can go to help you prepare an excellent business plan, in particular, the Small Business Administration. There are also many community development organizations that offer business planning courses that people can attend.

BOSTON: Do you have any suggestions for where to go when the banks say no?

COLEMAN: What a lot of people don't realize is that there are micro loan programs as well. Many times the program will make loans from $5,000 up to $25,000. Some even go higher; $35,000 or $50,000. The programs are not regulated like banks, so they can be a little more creative in putting together a financing request for you.

BOSTON: Now, have you seen anybody get any type of equity injection in addition to loans?

COLEMAN: Equity financing is kind of a different animal than debt financing and I think it's important for people to understand if they're looking for equity financing in the way of either angel investing or venture capital investing that they really need to do their homework. Equity investors are looking to make money and they want to make it quickly.

BOSTON: Let's talk about risk.

COLEMAN: You really cannot expect to be successful in business unless you're prepared to take some risks—financial risks, career risks. You really have to think long and hard about where you are in your life and how you are going to provide for others who might be important to you.

BOSTON: Okay. Now what's the role of the SBA?

COLEMAN: The Small Business Administration really exists to help small businesses succeed. One great myth is that the Small Business Administration has money to lend. It is not a direct lender. What they provide on the financing side is a loan guarantee for a lender.

Owning a small business is a great way to increase your net worth. It is not for everyone. But in today's ever-changing business climate, everyone should at least understand it and consider it as a viable career option.

Understanding how small business enterprises grow can also tremendously reduce a person's fear of being self-employed. Now take a few moments to consider how you can enterprise your entrepreneurial dreams.

MASTER KEYS

Know

Wherever you see a successful business, someone
once made a courageous decision.

—*Peter Drucker*

Act

Consider business ownership as a viable opportunity.
Understand what makes a good business plan.
Visit the SBA.gov web site.
Understand the traits of successful business owners.

Believe

I have what it takes to become a successful entrepreneur!

CONCLUSION

BECOMING THE MILLIONAIRE NEXT DOOR

A rich man is nothing but a poor man with money.

—*W.C. Fields*

EMOTIONAL FACTOR:
Fear of Owning Property

One of the best books ever written about the wealth-building process is *The Millionaire Next Door* by Thomas Stanley and William Danko (Pocket Books, 1998). If you haven't read it, I suggest that you do so. No success library is complete without it.

What has made this book a national best seller for many years has been the research about the lives of so-called ordinary American millionaires. Basically, the facts reveal that typical American millionaires live a simple life, live beneath their means, are diligent savers and hard workers, and own their own businesses. We discussed many of these characteristics in this book.

Many people were so fascinated by the statistics in *The Millionaire Next Door* that they virtually missed the point of this classic wealth-building book, which is that in the United States almost any one can become the millionaire next door. The opportunities to own your own investments, financial plan, insurance, pension plan, home, and business are available to most everyone. Because the United States has no laws restricting our ownership of these wealth-building investments, we can acquire assets that will help us become the millionaire next door.

Undoubtedly, ownership of appreciating assets is the primary way people become millionaires. So the issue is not just owning a home or a mutual fund or a stock pension plan or a business. Millionaires do not own these assets just for the sake of ownership. They own them because, historically, these assets appreciate in value over time.

Many people can never become the millionaire next door—not because they don't want to be, but because they are afraid to own property. Needless to say, this fear can be dangerous to your financial health.

Yes, owning property of any sort comes with responsibilities such as upkeep (with real estate), employees (with business enterprises), and capital gains tax (with equity investments). Will the return on these investments be worth your fear of ownership?

I cannot guarantee you that they will. I can guarantee you that without owning such investments, the return on your investments portfolio, if you have one, will be far less. Owning property that appreciates can help you win the financial success game.

Owning the Pond

The importance of owning assets was made clear to me one hot summer evening in Cleveland, Ohio. I was there attending a convention when I heard Bishop T.D. Jakes of Dallas, Texas, share his version of the well-known maxim, "If you give a hungry man a fish, you will feed him for a day. If you teach a hungry man how to fish, you will feed him for a lifetime."

Jakes took this saying to a whole new level when he said to the audience, "If you show the hungry man how to buy the pond that is filled with fish, then he will never worry about being hungry again. And neither will his children or grandchildren, or great-grandchildren." This parable demonstrates the importance of ownership. In this case, ownership of the pond not only secures prosperity, but also eliminates the fear of poverty.

When people ask me how they can become financially successful, I always remind them that "it's all about owning the pond." Then I share the parable with them. As it relates to our fear of success, owning the pond (owning appreciating assets) can reduce your emotional stress and increase your financial success. Emotional success and financial success can neutralize fears. Financial success can repress a person's financial fears. Likewise, financial fear can repress a person's financial success. Because financial fear and financial success can counteract each other, it was important for us to explore mastering both in this book.

In each chapter of this book you were introduced to individuals who took the emotional journey from financial fear to financial freedom. You read about these peoples' financial journeys in the Case Study, Profile in Courage, and Millionaire in the Making sections. Most of the households referred to in the Case Study have taken steps that will help them win the financial success game. The Millionaire in the Making households have secured their financial dreams and many of the Profile in Courage households' net worth already exceed one million dollars.

While each of these individual's road to financial success is unique, each story represents millions of other Americans who have taken the same remarkable economic journey. The financial odysseys shared in this work represent the countless stories, yet untold, about the households who invested a small sum every month in a growth stock mutual fund that over the years became a million dollar nest egg.

This same financial experience was shared by thousands of individuals who maxed out their 401(k) plan or other self-directed retirement account. Nor should we forget the households whose net worth grew dramatically as the equity in their home increased dramatically. The real peoples' stories cited in this book also mirror the countless number of small business owners whose business earnings help join the ranks of the most affluent economic class in America.

Like the individuals mentioned in this book, many affluent Americans have used the wealth-building strategies in this book to reach their financial goals. Our libraries, web sites, bookstores, newsstands, magazine racks, and financial television programs are filled with information about financially successful Americans. If you review these accounts carefully, you will discover that many of these individuals made many financial mistakes. You will also discover that many affluent Americans are not any smarter or started out any richer than you.

How can such people become financially successful? They all found the courage to face their financial fears and embrace the financial success that they truly desired. You can follow in their successful financial footsteps if you use the information you learned in this book.

In the Introduction, you learned that pursuing financial success is similar in many ways to playing a game. Throughout this book, we have referred to this game as the *financial success game* or the *great financial game of life*. The Introduction stresses that it is important to learn how to master playing the great financial game of life.

In Chapter 1, you gained insight into the different types of financial anxieties. You also discovered the three master keys that can help you achieve emotional and financial success. The first master key is knowledge. This key reminds you to use knowledge to understand your financial fears and strategies. The second master key is action. This key reminds you to use action to move beyond your financial fears. The third master key is belief. This key reminds you to foster your belief in yourself, free enterprise, and a higher power to replace your fears. You also learned in Chapter 1 that your lifetime earning capacity shows that you are a "millionaire in the making." You understand that by managing your financial stress, you can secure your financial success.

In Chapter 2, you were encouraged to enhance your intellectual capital, protect your physical capital, and embrace your spiritual capital. Taking these steps will help you unlock the emotional and financial success that lies deep within you. Success, you were reminded, must be perceived internally before it can be achieved externally.

Chapter 3 focused on how financial planning can help you take control of your financial life. In Chapter 4, you were urged to take responsibility for your finances by managing your credit effectively. You learned in Chapter 5 how to become homeowners and move beyond your fear of change.

The lesson covered in Chapter 6 was that the best way to reduce your fear of losing investment capital is to learn all you can about your investments and start investing on a monthly basis. In Chapter 7, you learned that the fear of growing older is a foolish reason not to secure your retirement. Chapter 8 provided you with a review of how to protect your financial dreams despite your fear of mortality. The premise in Chapter 9 is that properly starting a business can diminish your fear of business failure.

In the Conclusion, we reviewed how the fear of owning property can hamper your efforts to become the millionaire next door. In every chapter, you have been reminded to use knowledge to refute your fears, action to overcome your fears, and belief to replace your fears.

Having completed this book, you have the knowledge you need to play the financial success game. You understand that by managing your financial stress, you can secure financial success.

Like many Americans you, too, have the financial wherewithal to become the millionaire next door. But the issue remains, do they have the emotional will to do so? If you want to become the millionaire next door you must be committed to the process. The chief executive officer of a major corporation explained the word committment by referring to a ham and egg omlette.

Financial Success Factors and Opportunities

Chapters	Success Factors	Opportunities
Introduction	Playing the financial success game	Learn to play the game
Chapter 1	Understanding your financial fears	Ability to face your fears
Chapter 2	Developing your human capital	Discover the success within
Chapter 3	Planning your financial future	Purchase a financial plan
Chapter 4	Managing your credit	Reduce consumer debts
Chapter 5	Becoming a homeowner	Build real estate equity
Chapter 6	Becoming a confident investor	Open mutual fund accounts
Chapter 7	Securing your retirement	Begin retirement savings
Chapter 8	Insuring your financial dreams	Protect and share good fortune
Chapter 9	Starting a business enterprise	Build business profits
Conclusion	Becoming the millionaire next door	Own appreciating assets and master playing the game

He explained "to make a ham and egg omlette you need a few eggs and several slices of ham. Keep in mind that the hen that laid the eggs was involved in this process. The pork that produced the ham was committed to the process. To become the millionaire next door you must become committed to the process. Many Americans do not have the internal resolve to become economically successful. Too many Americans still let their financial stress impede their financial success.

Russell Simmons is the godfather of rap music. This self-made multimillionaire achieved his success on his own terms. He turned a $2,000 loan from his mother into a $500 million fortune. Once on *Moneywise,* Simmons commented on the fear that keeps many people from reaching their goals. "Many people are afraid of failure. They're afraid to invest their time and energy in their dreams," he said.

Thankfully, you will not have to count yourself among this financially fear-driven lot. Assisted by the information in this book, you can use knowledge to understand your financial fears and strategies. You can use action to move beyond your fears and implement your strategies. Lastly, you can use your belief in yourself, free enterprise, and a higher power to replace your fears. You will then pursue your dreams with less anxiety because your financial success will reduce your financial stress.

Thomas J. Stanley, PhD, is an author, lecturer, and researcher who has studied the affluent since 1973. He has written several best-selling books including *The Millionaire Mind* (Andrew McMeel Publishing, 2001) and the previously mentioned *The Millionaire Next Door.* Based on his years of research, Stanley has identified more than 100 techniques that millionaires use to reduce their fears. According to him, some of their most widely used fear-reducing methods are "hard work, planning, being decisive, consulting skilled experts, regular exercise, and praying."

Taking these steps helps economically successful people win the "mind over fear" game, as Stanley calls it. Affluent individuals often win that game because they never allow their fears to control their minds. His findings underscore that fear-reducing techniques are widely used by millionaires. His research also demonstrates two other important facts: (1) Mastering your emotional and financial well-being can help you win the mind over fear game; and (2) mastering your emotional and financial well-being can help you become a millionaire and win the great financial game of life.

Implementing the emotional and financial management steps presented in this book will help you win the wealth-building game. Unforeseen financial situations may occur that temporarily interrupt the total implementation of your wealth-building plans. No one can predict what will happen in the future with the economy, the stock market, the housing market, or the company where you work.

But by reading this book, you are better prepared to emotionally and financially withstand any unforeseen economic turbulence that may come your way. So welcome the future. You can face it confidently. You will not be a frightened victim of your financial future. Instead, you will be a fearless victor. You have the courage to become the millionaire next door. You can successful play the great financial game of life because you know how to master your emotional and financial success.

We will end this literary odyssey the way we began it. Let's revisit the affirmation found in the Introduction that was written by Joseph Murphy. When you first read this affirmation you probably read it with a fearful and timid attitude about your financial future. Now having read this work, you should be able to read this affirmation with a courageous and confident attitude. This change in attitude will have a positive effect on the way you read this affirmation and the way you view your financial future.

Say this affirmation as you take your emotional journey from financial fear to financial freedom. Recall this affirmation when you are implementing the financial strategies found in this book. Doing so will help you strengthen your emotional resolve and appreciate your economic progress. Remember always that:

"You are one with the infinite riches of your subconscious mind. You are happy, healthy, wealthy and successful. Money flows to you freely, copiously and endlessly. You are always aware of your true self-worth. You use your talents and you are wonderfully blessed financially" (Joseph Murphy, *The Power of Your Subconscious Mind*).

When you started reading this book you were an anxiety-filled millionaire in the making. Now having successfully completed this literary journey, you are ready to implement the lessons learned and to confidently become the millionaire next door.

MASTER KEYS

Know

What do most self-made millionaires have in common? They have courage.

—*Thomas J. Stanley*

Act

Face your financial fears.
Master playing the wealth building game.
Protect your physical capital, increase your intellectual capital, and embrace your spiritual capital.
Implement the strategies in your financial plan.
Keep your credit report spotless.
Become a homeowner.
Become a confident investor.
Save for your dream retirement.
Insure your financial dreams.
Start a small business enterprise.
Buy and own appreciating assets.

Believe

I can become the millionaire next door!

FINANCIAL SUCCESS RESOURCE GUIDE

Chapter 1 Understanding Your Financial Fears

Books

Beyond Greed and Fear: Understanding Behavioral Finance and the Psychology of Investing by Hersh Shefrin (New York: Oxford University Press, 2002). Describes how aspects of psychology and human nature affect investors who are motivated by emotions such as fear, hope, greed, and over-confidence. The book includes dozens of examples of investment mistakes and analyzes them from a behavioral finance perspective.

The Couple's Guide to Love & Money by Jonathan Rich (Oakland, CA: New Harbinger Publications, 2003). Tips to avoid money-based conflicts and negotiate financial issues. The author, a clinical psychologist, begins with a self-assessment quiz for readers to determine their money personality and that of their partner and to use this information to communicate effectively. The second half of the book focuses on wealth accumulation. Quizzes and worksheets help personalize key concepts.

Money Harmony: Resolving Money Conflicts in Your Life and Your Relationships by Olivia Mellan (New York: Walker & Company, 1995). Includes a "money personality quiz" for readers to determine their money type (e.g., hoarder, spender, money monk, avoider) and learn its key characteristics. Also includes techniques for effective communication about money and resolving financial conflicts. (See www.moneyharmony.com for additional information.)

Overcoming Overspending: A Winning Plan for Spenders and Their Partners by Olivia Mellan (New York: Walker & Company, 1997). Financial conflict resolution strategies for couples in which one or both partners suffer from an addiction to spending. The book uses case studies, including the author's, to describe various emotions associated with spending money and healthy substitutes that can fulfill these emotions without spending. (See www.moneyharmony.com for additional information.)

Prince Charming Isn't Coming: How Women Get Smart about Money by Barbara Stanny (New York: Penguin Books, 1999). Strategies to help women increase their knowledge and confidence about managing money. It also includes anecdotes from the author's life and emotional issues surrounding money. The overriding message is that women must take responsibility for their personal finances.

For Richer, Not Poorer: The Money Book for Couples by Ruth Hayden (Deerfield Beach, FL: HCI Books, 1999). Provides strategies for couples to explore their money values, set joint financial goals, and develop a workable budget. The book also discusses successful financial communication strategies. Concepts are illustrated with case study examples from the author's financial consulting practice.

10 Smart Money Moves for Women: How to Conquer Your Financial Fears by Judith Briles (New York: McGraw-Hill, 1999). Describes common financial fears of women, such as fear of losing money and fear of following the advice of a poor financial advisor. The book covers financial topics from a woman's perspective, including financial goal-setting, budgeting, spending, insurance, saving and investing, and retirement savings plans such as IRAs. It also includes self-assessment quizzes.

Why Smart People Make Big Money Mistakes and How to Correct Them: Lessons from the New Science of Behavioral Economics by Gary Belsky and Thomas Gilovich (New York: Fireside Books, 2000). Explores the psychology of financial decision making and explains why so many people make irrational financial decisions. Common behavioral finance errors are described in this book with dozens of real-life examples.

Online Publications

Coping with Financial Fears (Joel Garfinkle)
www.dreamjobcoaching.com/articles/financial-fears.html
An eight-step plan to face the fear of loss of financial security.

Face Your Financial Fears (Dr. Judith Briles)
www.msmoney.com/mm/financial_health/articles/face_fears1.htm
Advice about five common financial fears of women: fear of being poor, of losing money, of looking stupid, of talking about money, and of making mistakes. The author puts a positive spin on each fear and challenges readers to take charge of their financial well-being.

Facing Financial Fears (Lucynda Koesters)
www.stretcher.com/stories/01/010611c.cfm
Describes common financial fears, such as loss of investment capital and loss of a job, and strategies to face each fear with a positive action plan. Suggested strategies include establishing an emergency fund, selling assets to raise money for living costs, and waiting out market downturns.

Web Sites

Personal Resiliency Assessment Quiz (Rutgers Cooperative Research and Extension)
www.rce.rutgers.edu/money/resiliency
Provides users with an objective assessment of their personal resources for coping with stressful life events, including personal traits and financial, social, and community resources.

Chapter 2 Developing Your Human Capital

Books

Rags to Riches: Motivating Stories of How Ordinary People Achieved Extraordinary Wealth by Gail Liberman and Alan Levine (Chicago: Dearborn Financial Publishing, 2000). Profiles of 17 ordinary people who started with little and accumulated wealth over time. The authors also provide commentaries on strategies used by their subjects to accumulate wealth. Some of those profiled are household names such as pro golfer Chi Chi Rodriguez and poet Maya Angelou.

The Millionaire Mind by Thomas J. Stanley (Kansas City, MO: Andrews McMeel Publishing, 2001). Insights into the thought patterns of millionaires using data from focus groups and a survey with over 700 respondents. Common threads are that many millionaires have a specialized area of expertise that is lucrative, long and stable marriages, and good consumer purchasing skills.

The 9 Steps to Financial Freedom: Practical and Spiritual Steps So You Can Stop Worrying by Suze Orman (New York: Three Rivers Press, 2000). Advises readers to face deeply rooted money fears resulting from prior life experiences. The book includes advice on financial topics as well as psychological exercises that explore readers' personal feelings toward money.

Secrets of Six-Figure Women by Barbara Stanny (New York: HarperBusiness, 2004). The strategies used and obstacles overcome by over 150 women with annual earnings of $100,000+. According to the author, "our state of mind, more than anything . . . determines our level of success." The book discusses the required change in mind-set and risks associated with career success.

Think and Grow Rich by Napoleon Hill (New York: Ballantine Books, 1987). Insights into the development of a "millionaire mind-set" and the discipline to take action to achieve life goals. A classic book on wealth building, the first sentence reads as follows: "TRULY, thoughts are things, and powerful things, when they are mixed with definiteness of purpose, persistence, and a burning desire for translation into riches, or other material objects."

Online Publications

Family Communications about Money (University of Georgia Cooperative Extension)
www.fcs.uga.edu/pubs/current/HACE-E-17.html
Strategies and worksheets for communication with family members about financial issues.

Web Sites

Financial Fitness Quiz (Rutgers Cooperative Research and Extension)
www.rce.rutgers.edu/money/ffquiz
A diagnostic self-assessment tool of financial strengths and weaknesses that includes 20 questions.

Moneywise with Kelvin Boston

www.moneywise.tv

The web site for the *Moneywise PBS Show* television that airs nationally on public television.

Chapter 3 Planning Your Financial Future

Books

The Budget Kit: The Common Cents Money Management Workbook (3rd ed.) by Judy Lawrence (Chicago: Dearborn Trade, 2004). Dozens of budgeting and financial planning worksheets including forms to record monthly income and expenses, financial needs and wants, child support payments, gift-giving lists, debt payments, credit card purchases, mail-order purchases, medical and dental expenses, household net worth, tax-deductible expenses, and more.

Homefile: Financial Planning Organizer Kit by J. Michael Martin and Mary E. Martin (Arnold, MD: Homefile Publishing, Inc., 2004). Includes 22 "category cards" that describe a financial record-keeping category (e.g., bank accounts, insurance, investments), as well as a 48-page handbook that describes how to set up and maintain household financial files. Designed to be placed into a hanging file folder, the category cards tell what documents should be saved and for how long. The kit also includes a "Quick-Find Index" that lists the location (category) of over 200 commonly used household documents.

Just Give Me the Answer$: Expert Advisors Address Your Most Pressing Financial Questions by Sheryl Garrett (Chicago: Dearborn Trade, 2004). Answers to more than 130 questions on financial planning topics, including budgeting, debt repayment, and cash flow management. The answers are provided by the author and her national network of financial planners who serve middle-income clients.

Live Well on Less than You Think: The New York Times Guide to Achieving Financial Freedom by Fred Brock (New York: Times Books, 2005). Dozens of strategies to reduce expenses and free up money to invest. Topics include reduction of debt, regional living costs, small economies, insurance, cars, and retirement.

Ordinary People, Extraordinary Wealth by Ric Edelman (New York: Harper-Business, 2001). Describes the common practices of a financial planner's 5,000 clients who became wealthy over time. Among the characteristics that led to their success were maxing out contributions to company retirement plans, investing small sums on a regular basis, and following a "buy and hold" investing policy.

Saving on a Shoestring: How to Cut Expenses, Reduce Debt, and Stash More Cash by Barbara O'Neill (Chicago: MJF Books, 2003). Over a dozen financial topics with an emphasis on freeing up money to save for future goals.

7 Money Mantras for a Richer Life: How to Live Well with the Money You Have by Michelle Singletary (New York: Random House, 2003). Discusses money-saving tips and savings strategies that were influenced by the author's upbringing. The emphasis is on frugality and long-term saving with small dollar amounts. Among the mantras that are discussed and illustrated with examples are "Sweat the small stuff," "Priorities lead to prosperity," and "If it's on your ass, it's not an asset."

Smart Couples Finish Rich: 9 Steps to Creating a Rich Future for You and Your Partner by David Bach (New York: Broadway Books, 2002). Describes strategies for couples to build wealth over time. Topics include money values and financial goal-setting, how to work together toward a common financial goal, tracking household expenses, and common financial mistakes of couples.

Your Money or Your Life by Joe Dominguez and Vicki Robin (New York: Penguin Books, 1999). Strategies to get out of debt, establish a savings program, reorder material priorities, and live well for less. The authors contend that many people spend so much time working that they never take time to examine their priorities. They urge readers to calculate the "life-energy cost" of working and to increase savings and reduce expenses to reach the "crossover point" when income from investment capital exceeds monthly expenses.

Online Publications

Build Your Savings (University of Arkansas Cooperative Extension)
www.uaex.edu/Other_areas/publications/HTML/FSHEC-43.asp
A worksheet to list financial goals and a table of time value of money factors to calculate the savings required for achieving them. Also included in this four-page publication is a list of strategies to find money to save and a worksheet to compare interest rates and terms of financial institutions.

College Savings Plans

www.savingforcollege.com and www.collegesavings.org
Information about state-sponsored 529 college savings plans.

Getting Started Saving and Investing (University of Missouri Extension)
http://muextension.missouri.edu/explore/hesguide/famecon/gh3520.htm
An overview of investing topics including saving versus investing, risk tolerance, and sources of risk.

Web Sites

About: Financial Planning

http://financialplan.about.com
Articles and resources on financial topics including budgeting, saving money, retirement planning, and taxes.

Certified Financial Planner Board of Standards, Inc.

www.cfp-board.org and www.cfp.net
Links to publications about the financial planning process and how to select a financial planner. Also describes the credentials held by financial advisors and lists links to nonprofit and governmental agencies that have financial planning information.

The Dollar Stretcher . . . Living Better for Less

www.stretcher.com
Suggestions for saving money, building wealth, and reducing household expenses.

Financial Planning Association (FPA)

www.fpanet.org

A "Public/Find a Planner" page for consumers to locate a financial planner in their geographic area. The web site's public pages also include financial calculators, articles, brochures, and checklists, as well as an "Ask a CRP® Professional" feature where users can e-mail a question to an FPA member.

Kiplinger's Personal Finance Magazine

www.kiplinger.com

Personal finance feature articles, commentary, financial calculators, and daily financial updates. Companion web site to *Kiplinger's Personal Finance* magazine, a monthly personal finance periodical.

National Endowment for Financial Education® (NEFE)

www.nefe.org

Information about financial planning topics, summaries of financial conferences, and publications and Web links for youths and adults.

Newlywed Finances

www.newlywedfinances.com

Articles that address financial planning issues encountered by newly married couples.

Women's Institute for Financial Education (WIFE)

www.wife.org

Reviews of personal finance books, feature articles on personal finance topics, online video clips, and archived WIFE e-newsletters, all designed to improve the financial expertise of women.

Chapter 4 Managing Your Credit

Books

Are You Being Seduced into Debt? Break Free and Build a Financially Secure Future by John Cummuta (Nashville, TN: Nelson Books, 2004). Describes how Americans are seduced into debt by the powerful combined forces of merchants, advertisers, media, and the credit industry. The book also discusses strategies to accelerate debt repayment.

Credit Scores and Credit Reports: How the System Works, What You Can Do by Evan Hendricks (Cabin John, MD: Privacy Times, 2004). A thorough examination of credit reporting and scoring systems. Topics include factors that affect credit scores, ways to improve credit scores, identity theft, the use of credit scores to raise interest rates and set premiums for property insurance, and the cost to consumers of credit report errors.

How to Get out of Debt, Stay out of Debt, and Live Prosperously by Jerrold Mundis (New York: Bantam Books, 1990). Methods to handle debt, with an emphasis on support services provided by Debtors Anonymous. The author, who was once thousands of dollars in debt himself, includes many anecdotes from his own life and those of others and describes debt-handling methods.

Pay It Down! From Debt to Wealth on $10 a Day by Jean Chatzky (New York: Portfolio Books, 2004). A plan where the average U.S. household with $8,000 of high-interest credit card debt can be debt free in three years by repaying $10 more a day. The book describes dozens of debt reduction strategies to free up cash including expense reduction, debt consolidation, and selling assets. (See www.PayItDown.com for additional information.)

Slash Your Debt: Save Money and Secure Your Future by Gerri Detweiler, Marc Eisenson, and Nancy Castleman (Sun Lakes: Bookworld, 1999). How overextended consumers can repay what they owe quickly and cost effectively by increasing minimum payments on credit cards, consolidating debts, transferring credit card debt to a secured bank loan or home equity loan, and getting help from a credit counseling agency. (See www.goodadvicepress.com/syd .htm for additional information.)

Zero Debt: The Ultimate Guide to Financial Freedom by Lynnette Khalfani (Advantage World Press, 2004). Strategies for getting out of debt by a formerly overindebted author. Topics include credit card interest rates and fees, legal rights for credit users, dealing with creditors and collection agencies, credit reports and scores, and lifestyle changes for improved financial security.

Online Publications

Federal Trade Commission (FTC, Web Site on Credit)
www.ftc.gov/bcp/conline/edcams/credit/index.html (Click on "For Consumers" and "Credit Cards and Consumer Loans")
Links to PDF files of dozens of FTC publications on credit topics that can be downloaded free of charge. Topics of publications include *Avoiding Credit and Charge Card Fraud, Choosing and Using Credit Cards, Cosigning a Loan, Credit and Divorce, Fair Credit Billing,* and *Ready, Set . . . Credit.*

Purdue Extension Publications on Credit
www.ces.purdue.edu/extmedia/cfs.htm
Ten free downloadable *To Your Credit* publications in PDF format. Topics include *Choosing the Best Credit Card, Deciding How Many Credit Cards You Need, Getting Rid of Credit Card Debt, Checking Your Credit Report, Controlling Your Holiday Credit Use,* and *Fixing a Poor Credit Rating.*

Selecting a Credit Card (Montana State University Cooperative Extension)
www.montana.edu/wwwpb/pubs/mt9802.html
Information needed for wise credit card decisions in a 10-page publication. Topics discussed include credit card terms, annual percentage rates, and computation of finance charges, credit card fees, and minimum monthly payments. Updated in 2004, it includes a Credit Card Comparison Chart. (Also available in print for $1 by calling 406-994-2721.)

Web Sites

Annual Credit Report
www.annualcreditreport.com
A free credit report from each of the three major credit bureaus—Equifax, Experian, and TransUnion—according to federal law. This centralized web site allows consumers to request a free report once a year from each of the national consumer credit-reporting companies. There is also information available on the web site to request a free annual credit report by telephone or mail.

CardTrak®
www.cardtrak.com or www.cardweb.com/cardtrak
Feature articles on credit-related topics, credit calculators, a credit glossary, questions and answers, reviews of credit products, and information about

credit cards with specific features (e.g., secured credit cards, low-interest credit cards).

Consumer Action

www.consumer-action.org

Archived articles on financial topics, including credit and credit cards. A highlight of the web site is the annual Consumer Action *Credit Card Survey,* which lists pricing information for major credit cards nationwide and reports on credit industry trends.

Equifax

www.equifax.com

Information about ordering a credit report from the national credit-reporting agency, Equifax. (Also available by calling 800-685-1111.)

Experian

www.experian.com

Information about ordering a credit report from the national credit-reporting agency, Experian. (Also available by calling 888-397-3742.)

Federal Trade Commission (FTC)

www.ftc.gov/credit

Information about federal credit legislation, free annual credit reports, credit repair frauds, and other credit-related topics.

MyFICO

www.myfico.com

Information about credit scores. FICO® is an acronym for Fair Isaac & Company, the nation's leading provider of credit scores. The web site allows users to request their credit score for a fee and provides information about the factors that affect credit scores and how to improve them.

National Foundation for Credit Counseling

www.nfcc.org

Information about locating nonprofit consumer credit counseling service (CCCS) agencies and general credit and debt information.

PowerPay (Debt Reduction Analysis, Utah State University Cooperative Extension)

http://extension.usu.edu/cooperative/powerpay or http://powerpay.org

A debt reduction calendar and estimated time and cost savings for users who continue to pay the same amount to creditors monthly. When a creditor is repaid, the monthly payment that was previously paid is added to the monthly payment due to a remaining creditor. Users input their personal data (e.g., name of creditors, outstanding balance, monthly payment, and interest rate) for a personalized analysis.

TransUnion

www.transunion.com

Information about ordering a credit report from the national credit-reporting agency, TransUnion. (Also available by calling 800-888-4213.)

Television

The *Suze Orman Show* on CNBC is a general personal finance show where the host answers viewers' questions. Many of the inquiries are about credit and debt-related topics and suggested strategies are provided to overcome financial difficulties. The show airs several times on Saturday evenings.

Chapter 5 Becoming a Homeowner

Books

Financial Peace: Revisited by Dave Ramsey (New York: Viking Press, 2002). Personal anecdotes from the author, a national personal finance radio talk show host, who made money investing in real estate and lost it by age 30. The book describes the influence of money on family relationships and basic financial principles such as saving 10 percent of take-home pay, investing for the long-term with pretax dollars, and living below your means.

The One Minute Millionaire by Mark Victor Hansen and Robert G. Allen (New York: Harmony Books, 2002). Strategies to build wealth over time within the context of one-minute habits called "Millionaire Minutes." The book employs a self-help approach and includes fictional stories that illustrate specific techniques for creating wealth, such as tapping the power of leverage.

Rich Dad Poor Dad: What the Rich Teach Their Kids about Money That the Poor and Middle Class Do Not! by Robert Kiyosaki and Sharon Lechter (New York: Warner Business Books, 2000). Describes the primary author's financial upbringing through references to his father ("poor dad") and the father of a friend ("rich dad"). The book emphasizes entrepreneurship, the purchase of income-generating assets, and ongoing financial education.

Online Publications

Money 101 (*Money* magazine)

http://money.cnn.com/pf/101

A 23-lesson personal finance course from the writers at *Money* magazine. Users can read the entire course or choose lessons of interest. Topics include making a budget, basics of banking and saving, basics of investing, investing in stocks, investing in mutual funds, investing in bonds, buying a home, controlling debt, saving for college, kids and money, asset allocation, and taxes.

Web Sites

BankRate

www.bankrate.com

Current interest rates for home equity loans, mortgages, and certificates of deposit and financial calculators for mortgage payments, retirement savings, and other financial decisions. Also includes feature articles about financial planning, debt management, and credit topics.

Home Path (Fannie Mae)

www.homepath.com

A comprehensive resource about home-buying and financing topics.

HSH Associates

www.hsh.com

Loan payment calculators and archived feature articles about credit topics. This web site is especially useful as a "one stop shop" for mortgage loan rates for homebuyers. It also includes commentary and forecasts regarding interest rates and a question of the day regarding consumer lending.

Money Magazine
http://money.cnn.com or www.pathfinder.com/money
Information on general personal finance, including credit topics, as well as online calculators.

The Pocket Change Investor (Good Advice Press)
www.goodadvicepress.com/pci.htm
Suggestions for saving money, building wealth, and reducing household expenses.

Quicken Loans
www.quicken.com (Click on "Quicken Loans")
Online calculators to calculate potential mortgage payments, home loan articles, and rate quotes.

USA Today Money
www.usatoday.com/money
Current financial news, feature articles, financial calculators, and current CD and loan rates.

Chapter 6 Becoming a Confident Investor

Books

Eight Steps to Seven Figures by Charles B. Carlson (New York: Currency-Doubleday Books, 2000). Presents results of the author's research with over 200 everyday people whose investments made them millionaires. The book focuses exclusively on investing strategies and principles including financial goal-setting, investing regularly through dollar cost averaging, and tax-advantaged investing. (See www.thebusinesssource.com/aim/eightsteps .htm for additional information.)

The Four Pillars of Investing: Lessons for Building a Winning Portfolio by William J. Bernstein (New York: McGraw-Hill, 2002). Provides information about stock market history, investment risk tolerance, and asset allocation.

The Future for Investors: Why the Tried and True Triumph over the Bold and New by Jeremy Siegel (New York: Crown Business Books, 2005). Provides evidence, based on historical market returns, supporting the purchase of high-quality, dividend-paying stocks rather than trendy "hot" securities. The book provides a detailed historical perspective of stock-picking and investment asset-allocation strategies.

Investing for Dummies (3rd ed.) by Eric Tyson (Hoboken, NJ: Wiley, 2002). The basics of investing, including terminology, risks, and characteristics of investment products.

Investing on a Shoestring by Barbara O'Neill (Chicago: Dearborn Financial Publishing, 1999). Basic investing information for beginning investors with small dollar amounts to invest. Topics include developing an investor's mind-set, investment risk, and investment choices.

Pay Yourself First: The African American Guide to Financial Success and Security by Jesse B. Brown (New York: John Wiley & Sons, 2001). Describes financial topics related to making, spending, and saving money.

A Random Walk down Wall Street by Burton G. Malkiel (New York: W.W. Norton, 2004). Describes how difficult it is for investors to "beat the market" and the benefits of buying and holding a diversified portfolio with a core of index funds that mirror benchmark market indexes.

The Wall Street Journal Guide to Understanding Money and Investing (3rd ed.) by Kenneth M. Morris and Virginia B. Morris (New York: Fireside, 2004). Investment topics such as reading the financial pages, basic investment terms, and characteristics of securities such as bonds, stocks, mutual funds, and options.

When I Grow Up I'm Going to Be a Millionaire: A Children's Guide to Mutual Funds by Ted and Lora Lea (New Bern: Trafford Publishing, 2002). Teaches children (target ages 9 to 15) the basics of investing and personal finance within the context of a simple story. The two main characters discuss compound interest, the Rule of 72, characteristics of mutual funds, inflation, and the growth of investments over time. (See www.trafford.com for additional information.)

Online Publications

Beginners' Guide to Investing: Online Publications at the SEC (U.S. Securities and Exchange Commission)
www.sec.gov/investor/pubs/begininvest.htm
Links to over a dozen online investor education publications.

Investing for Success (National Urban League and Investment Company Institute Foundation)
www.ici.org/i4s/index.html
An interactive, multimedia online course on the basics of investing designed to strengthen investor awareness in the African American community. The course consists of 10 lessons with interactive quizzes, video clips, worksheets, brochures, and online calculators.

Investing for Your Future (Cooperative Extension System)
www.investing.rutgers.edu
An 11-unit basic investing home study course, an accompanying study guide, an investment glossary, and monthly messages on investing and related topics.

Smart Money University
www.smartmoney.com/university
Learning modules for both beginning and experienced investors.

Web Sites

Alliance for Investor Education
www.investoreducation.org
Information on investment-related topics including 401(k) plans, taxes, mutual fund fees, and selection of financial advisors.

CNBC
http://moneycentral.msn.com/investor/home.asp
Financial news, stock quotes, financial news articles, and more.

Investment Company Institute
www.ici.org
Information about mutual funds and fund investment companies.

Investment FAQ

www.invest-faq.com

Information about over a dozen investment-related topics.

Investor Education Fund: What's Your Risk Comfort Level?

www.investored.ca/en/interactive/quiz_risk_print.asp

An assessment of a user's investment risk tolerance.

MoneyCentral: How Much Risk Can You Handle?

http://moneycentral.msn.com/investor/calcs/n_riskq/main.asp

Provides an assessment of a user's investment risk tolerance.

Money Magazine

http://money.cnn.com

Daily financial updates, the *Money 101* financial planning course, financial calculators, real-time quotes, and articles about investing and general personal finance topics. Companion web site to *Money* magazine, a monthly personal finance periodical.

North American Securities Administrators Association

www.nasaa.org

Provides alerts about investment scams and contact information for state securities regulators.

Smart Money Magazine

www.smartmoney.com

Personal finance feature articles, commentary, financial calculators, and daily financial updates. Companion web site to *Smart Money* magazine, a monthly personal finance periodical.

U.S. Securities and Exchange Commission

www.sec.gov

Links to investment publications and online assistance with investing and investment fraud questions.

Television

CNBC provides daily business reports and commentary on investing and personal finance topics. Investors can learn about the financial markets through regular program segments with market-based titles such as Squawk Box, Power Lunch, Street Signs, and Closing Bell.

Chapter 7 Securing Your Retirement

Books

The Automatic Millionaire by David Bach (New York: Broadway Books, 2004). Describes a financially successful couple's automated strategies for wealth accumulation over time, including household expense reduction, the principle of "pay yourself first," automated retirement plan and investment deposits, and automated mortgage principal prepayments. (See www.finishrich.com/automaticmillionaire for additional information.)

Getting Rich in America: 8 Simple Rules by Dwight R. Lee and Richard B. McKenzie (New York: HarperBusiness, 1999). Describes research-based strategies to grow wealthy over time including planning with the future in mind, saving regularly from an early age, practicing frugal spending habits, getting a good education, staying married, practicing good health habits, taking prudent investment risks, and achieving life balance.

Make Your Paycheck Last: How to Create a Budget You Can Live With by Jason R. Rich (Franklin Lakes: Career Press, 2004). Step-by-step instructions to manage personal finances and to stop living paycheck to paycheck. Among the topics covered are developing a personalized budget that includes saving for future financial goals, debt repayment, and reducing household expenses.

Pocket Idiot's Guide: Living on a Budget by Peter Sander and Jennifer Basye Sander (New York: Alpha Books, 1999). Describes budgeting in simple terms using numerous sidebars and text boxes to present information. Topics include how to develop and follow a budget, budget categories, debt repayment, and purchasing big-ticket items.

The Wealthy Barber by David Chilton (Rocklin, CA: Prima Publishing, 1997). Teaches readers to achieve financial independence with practical advice provided by a fictional barber named Roy Miller. Topics covered include Roth IRAs, home buying, mutual funds, compound interest, investment strategies, and methods for saving money and achieving wealth over time.

Online Publications

Building Wealth: A Beginner's Guide to Securing Your Financial Future (Federal Reserve Bank of Dallas)
www.dallasfed.org
Presents four steps to wealth building over time with dozens of illustrations and simple worksheets. The four steps are to learn financial language, budget to save, save and invest, and take control of debt. Topics include net worth, budgeting, compound interest, and types of investments. (Also available by calling 800-333-4460, extension 254.)

Cutting Costs (Virginia Cooperative Extension)
www.ext.vt.edu/pubs/family/354-155/354-155.html
A six-page overview of dozens of expense reduction strategies as part of the budgeting process.

Developing a Spending Plan (Montana State University Extension Service)
www.montana.edu/wwwpb/pubs/mt9703.html
An eight-page, step-by-step description of the budgeting process with worksheets to balance income and expenses and include savings for future financial goals.

Guidebook to Help Late Savers Prepare for Retirement
www.nefe.org/latesavers/index.html
A downloadable 51-page booklet that includes over a dozen catch-up strategies for middle-aged savers who are trying to make up for lost time and prepare for retirement. Among the strategies described are increasing retirement savings deposits and changing investment asset allocation.

Savings Fitness: A Guide to Your Money and Your Financial Future
www.dol.gov/pwba/pubs
Describes how to build wealth over time including financial goal-setting, net worth, estimating retirement savings, debt and credit, compound interest,

employer savings programs, coping with financial crises, and selecting financial advisors. (Also available by calling 800-998-7542.)

Savings Plan Worksheet (Iowa State University Cooperative Extension)
www.extension.iastate.edu/publications/PM1462B.pdf
A worksheet and table of compound interest factors to help users estimate the monthly savings needed to reach a financial goal. An example is provided of saving $10,000 for a car in five years, which requires $154 of monthly savings at 4 percent interest. The worksheet can be used to determine the savings required to become a millionaire based on the user's time frame and investment earnings.

You First: A Guide for Baby Boomers
www.nefe.org/youfirst
A series of five handbooks that address retirement planning concerns of baby boomers with suggested strategies such as doing a financial checkup, setting and prioritizing goals, finding money to save and invest, calculating retirement savings needs, and planning for long-term care.

Web Sites

America Saves
www.americasaves.org
Information about savings topics such as finding money to save, building wealth through home ownership, and the awesome power of compound interest. Information is also provided about local savings campaigns that have been organized by states and cities across the country.

American Association of Retired Persons (AARP®)
www.aarp.org and www.aarp.org/moneyguide and www.aarp.org/finance
Several comprehensive web sites targeted to users age 50+ that contain material on a wide range of later life financial issues such as saving for retirement, estate planning, and long-term care.

American Savings Education Council/Choose to Save Partnership
www.asec.org (Click on "Savings Tools") and www.choosetosave.org
Downloadable publications and interactive online tools such as the *Ballpark Estimate* retirement savings worksheet, the *Retirement Personality Profiler,* and financial planning calculators.

Armchair Millionaire

www.armchairmillionaire.com

Feature articles on topics designed to help users achieve financial independence.

BankRate Budgeting 101

www.bankrate.com/brm/calc/Worksheet.asp

An online budget calculator that tells users how their spending compares with others in their same income bracket using national averages from the Bureau of Labor Statistics. Users are prompted to enter their monthly expenses for categories such as food, clothing, housing, and transportation.

Financial Engines

www.financialengines.com

Interactive retirement planning analyses that calculate the probability of users outliving their financial assets based on asset allocation and historical market returns.

Financial Security in Later Life (Cooperative Extension System)

www.csrees.usda.gov/fsll (Click on "Tools for Consumers.")

Links to online financial education resources with a focus on planning for retirement and later life issues such as long-term care.

Good Advice Press: How to Retire a Multimillionaire

www.goodadvicepress.com/finplan.htm

Describes steps to take charge of your financial life from the authors of the book *Invest in Yourself: Six Secrets to a Rich Life.* Their advice includes getting out of debt, setting priorities, paying yourself first, diversifying investments, increasing financial knowledge, and purchasing adequate insurance.

My Money.Gov (Financial Literacy and Education Commission)

www.mymoney.gov

Financial information in English and Spanish from federal government agencies on personal finance topics such as saving and investing. Users can download these publications from the links provided and can also order a free *My Money Toolkit,* sent via U.S. mail.

Planning for a Secure Retirement

www.ces.purdue.edu/retirement

A distance learning course on wealth accumulation and retirement planning that consists of 10 lessons and dozens of interactive links to calculators (e.g., for life expectancy) and other resources.

Retirement Personality Profiler (American Savings Education Council)

www.asec.org/profiler

An interactive self-assessment quiz that classifies users into one of five distinct retirement planning personalities (e.g., savers, deniers).

Social Security Administration

www.ssa.gov

Online calculators, contact information, and publications about Social Security.

Chapter 8 Insuring Your Financial Dreams

Books

The Finish Rich Workbook: Creating a Personalized Plan for a Richer Future by David Bach (New York: Broadway Books, 2003). A 10-step action plan to help readers take action on financial goals following the mantra, "Learn it, write it, live it." Topics include personal attitudes toward money, financial record keeping, values and goals, expense and debt reduction, the "pay yourself first" concept, insurance, low-cost investments, and selecting financial advisors.

The Richest Man in Babylon by George S. Clason (New York: Signet Books, 1955). Teaches wealth-building principles within a story about fictional characters set in ancient Babylon. Two middle-aged men seek the advice of Arkad, a wealthy Babylonian. Principles covered include saving 10 percent of earnings, controlling spending, investing wisely, and purchasing adequate insurance.

Ten Steps to a Better Financial Future (Washington, DC: American Association of Retired Persons, 2001). Ten strategies that women can follow to secure a better financial future. Topics include financial goal-setting, record keeping, budgeting, investing, insurance, and legal issues.

Tips from the Top: Targeted Advice from America's Top Money Minds by Edie Milligan (New York: Alpha Books, 2003). Hundreds of short paragraphs of advice about 14 personal finance topics from over 100 leading financial experts. Topics include portfolio management, income taxes, insurance, retirement and estate planning, saving strategies, children and money, housing and mortgages, credit, and budgeting.

Online Publications

How Much Am I Worth? (Rutgers Cooperative Research and Extension)
www.rcre.rutgers.edu/pubs/publication.asp?pid=FS012
A worksheet to calculate net worth (assets minus debts) and track wealth-building progress over time. A description of the benefits of calculating net worth is also included.

Wi$e Up: A Financial Planning Handbook for Generation X Women (U.S. Department of Labor)
www.wiseupwomen.tamu.edu/index.php
A 9-unit financial course targeted toward women in their 20s through early 40s. The publication includes nine chapters and a glossary. Each chapter contains worksheets for readers to apply information to their lives. The overall message is that it is never too soon to start planning for the future.

Web Sites

FinanCenter

www.financenter.com
Contains dozens of financial calculator tools for consumers on financial planning topics such as car buying, college planning, credit cards, IRAs, life insurance, saving, and retirement planning.

iVillage

www.ivillage.com
Articles written for women on financial topics such as budgeting, debt, saving and investing, insurance, and home ownership. Also includes interactive message boards where community members can support each other, provide suggestions, and give positive feedback.

Kiplinger's Personal Finance Budget Tool

www.kiplinger.com/personalfinance/tools/budget

Enables users to compare actual and projected expenses for major categories of household spending.

MSN.Money

www.moneycentral.msn.com

Daily financial updates and stock quotes and feature articles on financial topics such as insurance, credit, income taxes, and college and retirement planning.

Mvelopes

www.mvelopes.com

A commercial online budgeting system that enables users to pay bills and set up a record-keeping system with different expense categories and the ability to track the balance in each.

Nolo Press

www.nolo.com

Information about financial and legal topics such as debt repayment and estate planning.

Chapter 9 Starting a Business Enterprise

Books

Automatic Wealth: The 6 Steps to Financial Independence by Michael Masterson (Hoboken, NJ: John Wiley & Sons, 2005). Wealth-building tips for entrepreneurs and discussion of the importance of a positive attitude and expectations about wealth building. The author tells readers they must change habits and devote time to financial goals. While wealth building won't happen "automatically," it can be achieved over time.

The Millionaire Next Door by Thomas J. Stanley and William D. Danko (New York: Pocket Books, 2000). Presents the results of dozens of interviews over 20 years with self-made millionaires to discover their steps to wealth building. Specific strategies include living below one's means, adopting thrifty spending habits, saving 15 percent of pretax income, and being committed to hard work, sacrifice, and discipline.

Online Publications

Small Business Management Series (U.S. Small Business Administration)
www.sba.gov/library/pubs.html
Links to dozens of online publications about small business ownership.

Web Sites

Federal Citizen Information Center
www.pueblo.gsa.gov
An online source of federal government publications, including personal finance topics.

First Gov
www.firstgov.gov
A one-stop web site for information and services provided by federal government agencies.

Personal Budgeting and Money Saving Tips
www.personal-budget-planning-saving-money.com
Explains what a budget is and guidelines to create a workable plan. The web site includes links for subtopics such as cash flow, spending leaks, money-saving tips, and self-control.

Saving versus Spending Calculator (Readers Digest)
http://partners.leadfusion.com/tools/readersdigest/savings13/tool.fcs
Calculates how much money users can save over time through small changes to spending patterns (e.g., waiting to buy a new car, eating out less, paying off credit cards).

Wall Street Journal
www.wsj.com
Personal finance feature articles and daily financial updates. Companion web site to the *Wall Street Journal,* a daily personal finance newspaper.

ABOUT THE AUTHOR

Kelvin E. Boston is the executive producer and host of the *Moneywise with Kelvin Boston* public television series. An official PBS (Public Broadcasting Service) series since 2000, *Moneywise* is considered public television's longest running multicultural financial affairs television series.

In addition to airing on public television stations, *Moneywise* also airs on the American Forces Television Network where it reaches military households in 177 countries around the world. Kelvin Boston's first public television special entitled *Who's Afraid to Be a Millionaire?* premiered on public television stations in 2006.

Kelvin Boston is a popular public speaker. He speaks annually before government agencies, corporations, and nonprofit associations. In 2005, Boston received the "Communicator of the Year" award from the National Association of Market Developers. In 2003, Kelvin Boston was awarded the National Community Reinvestment Coalition's (NCRC) annual award for promoting economic justice.

Kelvin Boston is also the author of the best-selling book, *Smart Money Moves for African Americans* (Putnam 1995). Kelvin Boston is a graduate of Lincoln University (Lincoln, Pennsylvania) and a former regional financial planning manager for a national financial planning company.

Kelvin Boston is a respected television financial journalist, public speaker, and best-selling author who believes that financial education is the key that unlocks the door to financial success. To watch a video clip of the *Who's Afraid to Be a Millionaire?* television special featuring Kelvin Boston, please visit his web site at www.moneywise.tv.

INDEX